T0328879

Cambridge Elements ≡

Elements in Religion and Violence
edited by
James R. Lewis
University of Tromsø
Margo Kitts
Hawai'i Pacific University

ISLAM AND VIOLENCE

Khaleel Mohammed
San Diego State University

CAMBRIDGE
UNIVERSITY PRESS

CAMBRIDGE
UNIVERSITY PRESS

University Printing House, Cambridge CB2 8BS, United Kingdom

One Liberty Plaza, 20th Floor, New York, NY 10006, USA

477 Williamstown Road, Port Melbourne, VIC 3207, Australia

314–321, 3rd Floor, Plot 3, Splendor Forum, Jasola District Centre,
New Delhi – 110025, India

79 Anson Road, #06–04/06, Singapore 079906

Cambridge University Press is part of the University of Cambridge.

It furthers the University's mission by disseminating knowledge in the pursuit of
education, learning, and research at the highest international levels of excellence.

www.cambridge.org
Information on this title: www.cambridge.org/9781108728232
DOI: 10.1017/9781108610407

First published 2019

A catalogue record for this publication is available from the British Library.

ISBN 978-1-108-72823-2 Paperback
ISSN 2397-9496 (online)
ISSN 2514-3786 (print)

Cambridge Elements

Islam and Violence

Khaleel Mohammed

San Diego State University

ABSTRACT: After 9/11, many writers have posited that the relationship between Islam and violence is either elemental or anomalous. Khaleel Mohammed describes Islam as transcending the usual understanding of religion, being instead like a "sacred canopy" that provides meaning for every aspect of life. In addition, he shows that violence has both physical and psychological dimensions and expounds at length on jihad. He traces the term's metamorphosis of meaning from a struggle in any worthy cause to war and to its present-day extension that include martyrdom and terrorism. Finally, he covers the dimensions of violence in Islamic law and institutional patriarchy.

KEYWORDS: Islam, violence, jihad, patriarchy,

ISBNs: 9781108728232 (PB), 9781108610407 (OC)
DOI: 10.1017/9781108610407

Contents

Introduction

Religion is an ambiguous, amorphous term. For many, however, religion remains the foundation of morals, justice, peace, and everything that is good. Since peace and violence cannot be bedfellows, it would seem then that religion is the very antithesis of violence. In the wake of 9/11, however, the connection between religion and violence seemed indisputable – but then some researchers theorized that it is incorrect to see religion qua religion as the true source of violence. Several other issues, among which might be a fight against colonialism, foreign occupation, economic inequality, opposition to globalization – none of which is specifically "religious" – may be the more likely causes (Juergensmeyer, Kitts, and Jerryson 2013: 2). Worse yet, it might be that "religion" is being othered, in our enlightened times, as inferior to modern secularism. As William Cavanaugh eloquently puts it,

> The myth of religious violence helps to construct and marginalize a religious Other, prone to fanaticism, to contrast with the rational, peace-making, secular subject. This myth can be and is used in domestic politics to legitimate the marginalization of certain types of practices and groups labelled religious, while underwriting the nation-state's monopoly on its citizens' willingness to sacrifice and kill. In foreign policy, the myth of religious violence serves to cast nonsecular social orders, especially Muslim societies, in the role of villain.
> (Cavanaugh 2009: 4)

Government agencies such as the FBI and CIA that use speakers who make no secret of their anti-Muslim agenda only add to the marginalization of Muslims and the singling out of Islam as more prone to violence than other religions. The effect of such demonization is clear from polls. For example, in a December 2017 Pew Research Center poll, 41% of Americans deemed Islam as more likely than other religions to promote violence among its followers (Pew Research Center 2017).

It is important to note, however, that even those who speak of the connection between religion and violence as a myth do not deny that religion can be and is used to promote violence (Cavanaugh 2009: 5). While adherents to the different faiths may claim that those who resort to violence (and here, *violence* implies physical injury) do not truly understand their religion, the problem is that – especially in Islam – the explanation is simply incorrect. The Qur'an is very clear, for example, on the aspect of fighting for God when ordered as in Qur'an 2:216: "Fighting is enjoined upon you, but you dislike it. Yet, it may be that you hate a thing while it is good for you; or that you like a thing, and it is bad for you. God knows – and you know not."

One may argue that the Qur'an's verses refer to a specific situation, and that to cite them without reference to context would merely be creating a pretext. The history of Islam, however, forces us to observe three truths. The first is that once a religion becomes state doctrine, it will necessarily lead to what Max Weber termed "bureaucratization" and "routinization" (Weber 1991: 224). Unlike Christianity, which took four centuries to become a state religion, Islam was married with political power during the lifetime of its founder. Muhammad, as prophet and statesman in Medina, promulgated rules and regulations that controlled the entire community. After his death, the formation of the caliphate and the selected reading of the Qur'an and prophetic traditions to frame a law of nations (*ahkām al-siyar*) often led to wars that saw the building of an empire.

The second truth is that once religion forms the basis of law, a theocracy exists, opening the door for totalitarian interpretations of what is right. The routinization of law may often lead to the loss of ethical assessment, especially after the death of the founder of the religion, when his charisma is no longer there; authority then comes via the viewpoints of his successors. In the case of Islam, the caliphs, and later the jurists, exercised this authority. The third truth is somewhat related to the second: if there is a weak central government, groups may exert their influence in the name of religion to discriminate against minorities. This is clearly evident in places like Pakistan where groups like Sipah Sahaba Pakistan (SSP) and Lashkar Jhangvi terrorize Shia Muslims, Christians, and Ahmadiyya Muslims (Saeed, Martin, and Syed 2014).

It is necessary to provide working definitions of "Islam" qua religion and "violence" if I am going to write an entire Element on the connection between the two. Religion as a self-evident construct is essentially a post-Enlightenment Western creation (Cavanaugh 2009; Smith 1991). While some may agree with Charles Kimball's view that, even though there is no consensus on the definition of religion, we nonetheless know religion when we see it (Kimball 2002: 15), others convincingly argue that there is no neat divide between the secular and the religious. Indeed, the very term *secular* evolves out of Christian theology (Asad 1993: 207; Casanova 2011: 56; Derrida 2001: 67). For many Muslims, this is in line with the understanding of Islam qua religion since Qur'an 6:162 enjoins Muslims thus: "Say: My prayers, my rituals, my life and my death are for God, Lord of all the Worlds."

The term *Islam* is derived from the Arabic root *SaLiMa*; most definitions, however, translate that as "peace" or "submission," overlooking that the word also means "to be perfect" (see, for example, Denny 1985: 67 and al-Dawoody 2011: 47). I argue that a more accurate meaning is from the

Qur'anic version of Genesis 17:1, where God orders Abraham to seek perfection. The Hebrew imperative תָּמִים (*Tamim*) had become שְׁלִים (*Shlaim*) in the Targum, a rendition that the Arabs would have more likely known. Qur'an 2: 131–132 summarizes the event, using the Arabic cognate for the imperative of the Targum:

> The Lord said to him: Be perfect أسلم (*aslim*). He answered: I turn my face for perfection to God. And he counselled his sons, as did Jacob. "Oh, my children! Indeed, God has chosen for you a path; do not die unless you are in this state of perfection."

Islam, then, has to do with seeking perfection based on interpretations of the Qur'an and tradition, forming the connection between Muhammad's message and God's order to Abraham to form a community of believers (see Donner 2010). For the purposes of this Element, Islam is a "sacred canopy" (see Berger 1990) that gives meaning and authority to what Muslims may deem necessary to fulfill that seeking of perfection, be it in ritual, personal conduct in society, or, indeed, in all aspects of life. In today's world of nation-states, where secular manifestos are the norm, Muslim-majority states such as Saudi Arabia and Pakistan exemplify that "sacred canopy" imagery, either by claiming to operate under purely religious law or by proclaiming "islamization" to rely heavily on religion in governance.

Insofar as violence goes, the general idea is to think of the shedding of blood, martyrdom, or the "jihadism" that so many see as elemental to Islam. The meaning is much wider (Juergensmeyer et al. 2013: 2), and to incorporate that broader sense, I use Craig Nessan's definition: "the attempt of an individual or group to impose its will on others through any nonverbal, verbal, or physical means that inflict psychological or physical injury" (Nessan 1998: 451).

In the context of this Element, the violence is exerted by those who act or are perceived as acting in the name of Islam, using language and symbols derived from authoritative texts and traditions to bring about physical damage or gender discrimination or to promote an "us" against "them" binary.

Islam contains so many juristic and interpretational differences that scholars generally acknowledge that there are several Islams. I choose not to detail such differences in this Element and embark on a sort of essentialism. Since the Sunnis constitute approximately 85–90% of the world's Muslim population, I refer mainly to Sunni books and interpretations. I have divided this Element into five sections: Introduction, Jihad, Islamic Law, Patriarchy, and Conclusion. For the sake of simplicity, I avoid the use of diacritics except where vital. All translations, unless I indicate otherwise, are my own.

From Jihad to War to Terrorism

After 9/11, *jihad* has become the most discussed term in debates about Islam (Bonner 2006: 1; Lawrence 1998: 1). The following examples make the reason obvious: 9/11, 7/7, and 26/11; the shoe bomber; the Brussels metro and airport; Manchester, London, Paris, and Barcelona; the Boston Marathon bombing; suicide bombers in Afghanistan, Pakistan, Iraq, Syria, and Israel; al-Qaeda and ISIS. Whether the foregoing refer to horrific acts or terrorist organizations, they generally evoke the image of Muslims carrying out some form of jihad.

In seeking to enlighten us about the violent proclivity of Muslims, Sam Harris tells us:

> Subtract the Muslim belief in martyrdom and Jihad, and the actions of suicide bombers become completely unintelligible, as

does the spectacle of public jubilation that invariably follows their deaths; insert these particular beliefs, and one can only marvel that suicide bombing is not more widespread.

(Harris 2004: 33)

While many of Harris's conclusions are questionable, he can find support in some academic writings for his claim about the warlike nature of Islam. Long before 9/11, for example, Orientalist scholar Emile Tyan (d. 1977) wrote about jihad (rendered as "djihad") in *The Encyclopedia of Islam*:

The notion stems from the fundamental principle of the universality of Islam: this religion, along with the temporal power which it implies, ought to embrace the whole universe, if necessary by force ... the *Djihad* is not an end, but a means which, in itself, is an evil (*fasad*) but which becomes legitimate and necessary by reason of the objective towards which it is directed: to rid the world of a greater evil; it is good from the fact that its purpose is greater.

(Tyan 1960: 2:538–539)

Tyan's words seem designed to foster a particular conclusion: jihad is evil, and the God of the Qur'an is ordering Muslims to commit evil. Writers like Tyan and Harris use carefully chosen sources, deliberately obfuscating any material that might contradict or debunk their conclusions. Tyan, for example, limited himself to the post-prophetic legal writings that present jihad primarily as fighting and as a duty, not considering that such material came in a particular time and context. Sam Harris's deliberate decontextualization of verses of the Qur'an is because he wishes to denigrate rather than engage in objective analysis of a subject that is not his specialty.

Bernard Lewis admits that the literal meaning of *jihad* is "effort" or "struggle," but then somehow jumps to the conclusion that its usage in the Qur'an means "to wage war" (Lewis 1988: 72).

> The basis of the obligation of Jihad is the universality of the Muslim revelation. God's word and God's message are for all mankind; it is the duty of those who have accepted them to strive (*jahada*) unceasingly to convert or at least to subjugate those who have not. This obligation is without limit of time or space. It must continue until the whole world has either accepted the Islamic faith or submitted to the power of the Islamic state.
>
> (Lewis 1988: 73)

He mentions one dissenting voice – that of Sufyan al-Thawri – and omits to mention that early Islamic discourse involved several different opinions (Mottahadeh and al-Sayyid 2001: 23–29).

Contrary to what Tyan and Lewis would have us believe, there has never been any single Islamic creed or law about jihad, since there is no singular authoritative body in Islam. All we have from Muslim writers throughout the ages are numerous legal opinions that may all be equally "normative" (Mottahadeh and Sayyid 2001: 23–29; see also Abou El-Fadl 2007: 21–22; Afsaruddin 2015: 70–81).

Many Muslims argue that to see jihad solely as war is a horrible misrepresentation of the Islamic *weltanschauung*. Some even contend that the true meaning of jihad is to seek spiritual self-improvement (Kabbani and Hendricks n.d.). This position, however, is just as misleading as the one it opposes, relying on similar casuistry albeit to promote a different viewpoint. Many claim, for example, that the Prophet Muhammad himself instructed his followers that "the greater jihad" is about spirituality, while the "lesser jihad" is about armed conflict. The problem with this tradition (*hadith*) is that hadith specialists have debunked it.[1]

Several factors have influenced the various interpretations of the polyvalent "jihad." It seems clear that the concept is still evolving, seeking to adapt to the drastic changes of a present that is so vastly different from the milieu in which the term was first used (Hashmi 1996: 146–168). Nonetheless, it is quite surprising that *jihad* should have surfaced as the singular Islamic word, in modern times, to connote war and fighting when the Qur'an has specific terms (*harb*, *qitāl*) to denote such activities. Why have these other Arabic lexes, despite their specific etymological directness, not become the primary terms? Why is it that many calls for jihad by Muslims in various conflicts have been unsuccessful, and suddenly, at the end of the twentieth and the beginning of the twenty-first centuries, become so widely accepted? In this section, I answer these questions as well as provide a history of the evolution of the concept, from a polysemous term to a univocal "war" to modern-day interpretations that allow, in some cases, for outright terrorism.

The Arabs to whom Muhammad preached his message had long viewed tribal skirmishing as a normal activity. The paucity of resources in an area where no single state had control meant each tribe was a law unto itself, vying against others for existence, unless some pact or treaty established an alliance or détente. Raiding (*ghazw*) was frequent, regarded more as a simple fact of desert existence, or even as sport, although protocols were in place, governed by the concept of manliness (*muruwwa*),

---

[1] Ahmad Ibn Taimiyya considered the tradition baseless (2000: 11:197), and Muhammad Nasr al-Din al-Albani deemed it unreliable (2002: 5:478).

which extolled bravery, loyalty, and the dogged pursuit of vendettas, among other traits.[2]

This explains why Muhammad could survive the early years of his ministry although he faced hostile opposition. As a member of the Banu Hashim clan, he was under the protection of his uncle Abu Talib. When that uncle died, however, Muhammad and his family were ostracized and, along with his followers, endured a period of siege. His little band was powerless to fight back and it is in this light that we must understand the earliest usage of *jihad* in the Qur'an. The tripartite consonantal root *jhd* means "struggle," "striving," or "exertion" (Ibn Manzoor n.d.: 2:395–397). Words derived from this root occur forty-seven times in the Qur'an (in forty-one verses), with the lexeme "jihad" used thrice as a noun and once as an adverb. In many cases, it occurs with the conditional "*fi sabil Allah*," which would render the combined meaning as "struggling for the sake of God" (Afsaruddin 2007: 165–169).

The primary use of the term and its derivatives is to exert effort toward a commendable goal, including peaceful persuasion (Q16:125), passive resistance (Q13:22, 23:96, 41:34), oath-taking (Q5:53, 6:109, 16:38, 24:53, 35:42), and, in some cases, armed conflict (Q3:142; 4:95, 9:16, 24, 41, 44, 81, 85, 88; 61:11).[3] The overwhelming usage of *jihad*, then, does not indicate a necessary connection with armed or physical combat. As noted earlier, other words appear in the Qur'an for such activity, *harb* and *qitāl* being the prime examples. *Harb* is the functional Arabic term for "war" and occurs four times in the

---

[2] Fred Donner views it more as sport, not unlike the medieval chivalry of Western Europe (Donner 1991: 31–70). For *muruwwa*, see Majid Khadduri, *The Islamic Conception of Justice* (Khadduri 1984: 9).

[3] For a good discussion of the various meanings in the Qur'anic usage, see Abdul Haleem, *Qur'anic Jihad*.

Qur'an: in Q5:64, 8:57, 47:4 and in Q2:279. *Qitāl* is specifically used for fighting, and occasionally refers to a form of jihad.[4] Interestingly too, the Qur'an often presents *sabr* (patience and forbearing) as an essential component of jihad (Afsaruddin 2013: 3), but does not do so when referring to *harb* and *qitāl*. This point underlines the error of seeking to equate the scriptural or classical use of *jihad* to mean holy war, or the idea of subjugating the world to Islam (see Abou El-Fadl 2007: 222).

The earliest use of the term *jihad* is in its specific lexical sense of struggling toward an objective: one revelation in Mecca instructs that: "*jāhidhum bihi Jihādan kabīrā*" (Q25:52). The general interpretation of this verse is that Muhammad is to argue against his opponents by using the Qur'an. Although no fighting took place during this period (610–622 CE), a de facto state of war already existed (al-Dawoody 2011: 18), with the Muslims practicing passive resistance. When Muhammad and his followers fled Mecca in 622 CE, their Meccan enemies confiscated their land and properties (Alsumaih 1998: 191ff.). The Muslims did not just relocate from one place to another: they left as refugees of war. The desert lifestyle meant that the Muslims were now on their own, and that unless they could defend themselves, or ally with some powerful tribe, they would be destroyed.

Medina, to where Muhammad fled, was itself a troubled city, with several groups (many of which were Jewish) in conflict with each other. Unlike in other parts of Arabia, each group here was autonomous, not working under the concept of tribal alliances (al-Dawoody 2011: 19). This explains the importance of the "Constitution of Medina" (*Sahifah al-Medina*) that Muhammad and his followers entered into with the inhabitants of Medina. The gist of the pact was an alliance among the believers in the Abrahamic faiths

---

[4] *Qatala* and its derivatives occur 170 times, with the noun form, *qitāl*, used in thirteen cases.

to function as a single community, with Muhammad as the leader. The agreement further made Medina a sanctuary wherein bloodshed was forbidden and that was to be as sacred to its inhabitants as Mecca was to the Meccans. Interestingly, one clause of the Constitution of Medina reads thus: "This is a writing from Muhammad the Prophet between the believers and Muslims from Quraysh and Yathrib [Medina] and those who followed them, joined with them and *jāhad* with them that they are one *umma* (community or nation) from among the people" (al-Dawoody 2011: 20; Ibn Ishaq 1986: 2:85). It is important to note that at this stage, no fighting had yet occurred, and in context, the meaning is, in its lexical form, to indicate the exertion of effort to exist in harmony and as a single community. There is a strong focus on unity against perceived enemies because of the reality of the situation. At the same time, it was obvious that the Quraysh were far more powerful than the Medinites. In a place where he had newly settled, it is unlikely that Muhammad would have deliberately done anything to precipitate a full-scale war.

It was in Medina (i.e., after the year 622 CE) that the verses allowing and regulating warfare were revealed.[5] The overwhelming majority of exegetes opine that the first verses were Q 22:39–40:

> Permission is given to those against whom fighting has been initiated (*yuqātalūna*) because they have been wronged/ oppressed, and God is able to help them. They are they who have been wrongfully expelled from their homes merely for saying, "God is our Lord." If God had not restrained some people by means of others, monasteries, churches, synagogues, and mosques in which God's name is mentioned frequently

---

[5] Among these verses are, not in any chronological order: 2:190–194, 216–217; 4:75–76; 8:38–39; 9:29; 22:39, 40; 60:8–9.

would have been destroyed. Indeed, God comes to the aid of those who come to His aid; indeed, He is powerful and mighty.[6]

Some exegetes, such as al-Qurtubi (2000: 2:231) and Ibn Kathir (1980: 1:227), claim that the first revelations about war were in fact the following:

> Fight in the way of God those who fight you, but do not exceed the limits; indeed, God does not like those who exceed those limits. Fight them wherever you find them and expel them from wherever they expelled you. Persecution is more grievous than killing. Do not fight them at the Sacred Mosque unless they fight you there, but if they fight you, then kill them. Such is the recompense of the unbelievers. But if they desist, then surely, God is most forgiving, most merciful. Fight them until there is no persecution, and religion is for God. If they cease, then let there be no hostilities except against the persecutors. The Sacred month for the sacred month, and violations are subject to retaliation. Whomsoever therefore commits aggression against you, then respond against him in the same manner he has aggressed against you. But be God-conscious and know that God is with those who are God-conscious.
>
> (Q2:190–194)

This more detailed set of verses, i.e. Q2:190–194, actually refers to a specific incident. Most exegetes place this at about the time of the treaty of Hudaibiya reached between Muhammad and the Quraysh in 628 CE. Both sets of verses, regardless of their chronological order, show four things: (a) they do not

---

[6] Translation as rendered by Asma Afsaruddin (2017).

allow the Muslims to initiate war; (b) they exhort Muslims to observe protocols regarding what is allowable in conflict; (c) they prohibit fighting in sacred areas; and (d) they enjoin the cessation of fighting if the enemy desists.

Several circumstances dictated the tone and injunctions of the subsequent revelations on war. The kinship relations between the warring parties may have made some reluctant to do battle. The proscription of fighting in certain months too would mean that the Quraysh might attack without fear of reprisal. Simple cowardice, as well as the harsh reality of statistics, may have also played a role: the Quraysh were strong and the vast number of warriors they could put in the field with their superior resources would have made ultimate victory for Muhammad's group seem almost impossible. As such, the following conditioning verses were revealed:

> Fighting has been enjoined upon you, and it is hateful to you. But it is possible that you may hate something even though it is good for you. You may like something, and it is bad for you. God knows best, and you do not. They ask you about fighting in the sacred month. Fighting at that time is grave, but barring from God's way and rejecting God, expelling people from the sacred mosque are graver in God's reckoning. And persecution is worse than killing. They will persist in fighting you until they make you give up your religion if they are able. And whoever amongst you repudiates his religion, and dies as an unbeliever, such will have his deeds count in vain in this world and the hereafter. They will be denizens of the Fire, abiding therein forever.
>
> (Q2:216–217)

The Qur'anic edict allows treaties against those who do not persecute the Muslims. This is evident in verses like:

> God does not forbid you from dealing kindly and justly with those who did not fight you because of your religion nor expel you from your homes. Verily, God loves the just. But God forbids you from allying with those who fought you because of your religion and expelled you from your homes and aided and abetted in your expulsion. Whoever allies with such folk are wrongdoers.
>
> (Q60:8–9)

Anti-Islam polemicists usually rely on Q9:5, 29 as their evidence for an Islamic supremacist declaration of outright war against all non-Muslims. These verses, however, cannot be read independently and must be placed in context. Verse 9:5 – often known as the sword verse – states that:

> When the sacred months have passed, slay the idolaters wherever you find them; take them captive, and besiege them, and lay wait for them with every stratagem. But if they repent, establish worship and pay the zakat, then leave their way free. Behold! God is Forgiving, Merciful.

The context of the chapter in general seems to indicate that the Quraysh had violated the treaty of Hudaibiya. This treaty, negotiated in 628, had allowed for a ten-year armistice, but the Quraysh violated its terms by allying with the Banu Bakr against the Banu Khuza'ah (al-Dawoody 2011: 28, 64). The first few verses were recited during the early days of the Pilgrimage in March 631, so that the Meccans who had no treaties with the Muslims could vacate the area.

The first verse of the chapter restricts its meaning to a specific group: "those with whom you have made agreements from amongst the polytheists." All subsequent verses are to be seen as restricted to this circumstance and are therefore not a license to open warfare as some later exegetes and Western-based researchers have suggested (see Abdel-Haleem 2010: 147–166).

Muhammad marched into Mecca in victory in 630 CE; by the time he died in 632, Islam was the dominant religion in the Arab peninsula. The record of the number of military engagements he engaged in is problematic because some of the words used, such as *ghazwa* or *sāriya*, may refer to a simple trip for intelligence, treaty making, a military foray, or even a worship ritual, such as the *'umra* (al-Dawoody 2011: 21ff.). What we do know is that about seven major battles were fought during Muhammad's lifetime: Badr, Uhud, Khandaq,[7] Khaybar, Fath Makka, Hunayn, and Tabuk.

Muhammad also fought battles against some of the Jewish tribes that had been signatories to the Constitution of Medina agreement. One such instance was the case of the Banu Qaynuqa that sided with the Quraysh at Badr and Uhud (al-Tabari n.d.: 364–365). Another tribe, the Banu Nadir, was relocated to Khaybar for not adhering to the terms of the Constitution of Medina and refusing to pay the blood money when some of its members killed two men from another tribe (al-Dawoody 2011: 26). The Banu Nadir then amassed a gathering of several clans, aided by 4,000 troops from the Quraysh, to attack Medina. This resulted in the famous Battle of the Ditch (*al-Khandaq*), in which a moat (*khandaq*) was dug to repel the attack. Another Jewish tribe, the Banu Qurayza, had aided in the attack on Medina, and after being besieged, agreed to the verdict of one of its allies, Sa'd ibn Muadh. As al-Dawoody observes, there

---

[7] Sometimes referred to as Battle of the Confederates (*Ghazwat al-Ahzāb*) in reference to the alliance that the Quraysh entered into with other tribes.

seems to have been no resistance to this sentence, most likely given that the sentence was in accordance with Jewish law as outlined in Deuteronomy 20: 10–15 (al-Dawoody 2011: 27). The total number of enemy killed in war during Muhammad's lifetime, then, even if one were to include the executed Banu Qurayza, would not exceed 1,000 (Abdel-Haleem 2010: 147–166). It is important to note too that the battles were not termed "jihad," and that the cause for conflict was not to impose Islam upon non-Muslims, but to fight against those who wanted to coerce the Muslims to renounce their new faith.

Muhammad died in 632, and without his authority and charismatic guidance, the cohesiveness of the *umma* was threatened. The earliest evidence of this is when some tribes threatened to secede from the Islamic polity, and not pay the *zakat*. Abu Bakr, the first caliph, fought such tribes in the *Ridda* wars, so named from the word meaning apostasy or secession. None of these internecine conflicts warranted the name "jihad." The names used for such conflicts were *ghazawāt*, *maghāzi*, *siyar*, and *futūh*. *Jihad*, if ever used for the period, is not a central theme of early Muslim conflict (Lawrence 2013: 133). The Islamic polity expanded rapidly and within ten years held sway over many of the lands of the Middle East. The successors of Muhammad engaged in internecine warfare for leadership of the Muslim state and ended up creating a dynastic system out of the caliphate, as indicated through the nomenclature of the "Umayyads" (661–750) and the "Abbasids" (750–1258).

Jihad as a theme in Islamic juridical and historical literature only came into post-prophetic prominence as the Islamic polity faced wars on the Byzantine frontier, and there was a need to find some scriptural or prophetic justification for such conflicts (Afsaruddin 2007: 165–169; Mottahadeh 2001: 26). It was during the caliphates of the Umayyad and early Abbasid dynasties that scholars suggested the division of the world into *"Dar al-Islam"* and *"Dar al-Harb,"* suggesting continuous enmity between the two entities based solely on religion. The term *jihad* lost its polyvalence, and fitting with the *realpolitik* of the period, came to be generally understood only in terms of fighting and war. Some jurists tried to obfuscate the clear context of the Qur'an and to claim that Q9:5, now deemed the "sword verse," had abrogated all previous *ayahs* that allowed for coexistence or treaties. By the eighth century, however, the Muslims focused more on consolidating territories under their control rather than seeking to conquer new frontiers (Hillenbrand 2000: 93). Both the Byzantine and Islamic polities engaged in practices that consisted largely of shows of power to appease their citizens rather than to embark on conquest missions (Hillenbrand 2000: 93).

Along with the refraction of jihad as being related to war only, the concept of martyrdom also became prominent. The Qur'an has no word for martyr or martyrdom; this concept only occurs in the hadith literature. Some exegetes do try to find a reference in Q2:154 (cf. 3:169; 47:4) that reads, "speak not of those who are killed in the path of God as dead; rather they are alive, but you do not perceive this." The exegetical and hadith works have shown, though, that the meaning of the verse is not restricted to those who have been killed in battle, and could refer to several other cases, such as, for example, one who dies in childbirth, or is drowned (Ibn al-Hajjaj 1992: 4:1059). The idea, as Asma Afsaruddin posits, most likely, is an imported one:

> It is telling that nowhere in the Qur'an is this word used for a martyr; rather it is only used, interchangeably with shāhīd to refer to a legal or eye witness. Only in later extra-Qur'anic tradition does this word acquire the specific meaning of "one who bears witness for the faith," particularly by laying down his or her life. Extraneous, particularly Christian, influence may be suspected here. Muslim encounters with Levantine Christians in

the late 7th century very likely contributed to this development. The cognate Syriac word for martyr-witness *Sahedo* may have influenced the Arabic *shahīd* and led to the latter's subsequent acquisition of the secondary and derivative meaning of "martyr."

(Afsaruddin 2016)

Throughout history, many Muslim leaders have used the galvanizing capacity of the word *jihad* to motivate their followers to action. The first important call was as a response to the Crusades (1096–1291). Mahmoud Mamdani notes that, until the Afghan jihad of the 1980s, there were only four widespread uses of the term as a mobilizing slogan (Mamdani 2004: 50ff.). In the following analysis, I accept this general structure, even though my discussion incorporates movements that he may not have discussed in the specific work in which he outlined this periodization.

The First Major Call: Response to the Crusades and Establishing the Ottoman Stronghold

At the Council of Clermont in November 1095, Pope Urban II announced that God had willed European Christians to go to battle to retake the Holy Land from Muslim control. This call precipitated a series of wars known as the Crusades, lasting until 1291. When Crusaders invaded Jerusalem in 1099, they found the Muslims were too preoccupied with their own internal squabbles to offer any united resistance. Rather, different Muslim leaders engaged in forming alliances with the Franks (as they called the Crusaders), and as such, it is somewhat incorrect to see the Crusades solely as a "Christian against Muslim" series of wars (Hillenbrand 2000: 20–21). A good example is shown in the Battle of Danith: the army that the Seljuk sultan, Muhammad, sent into Syria in 1115 was routed by an alliance of Crusaders and Muslims from factions that opposed him (Hillenbrand 2000: 20–21).

The Muslim forces only began to show resolve in expelling the enemy after Imad ad-Din Zangi (d. 1146) wrested Edessa from the Crusaders in December 1144. After Zangi's assassination, his son, Nur al-Din, took his place. By the time of his death in 1174, Nur al-Din had united the factions in Syria and made himself the supreme Muslim ruler. His lieutenant in Egypt, Salahuddin al-Ayyubi, defeated the rival armies of the Fatimid caliph in Egypt and abolished that office in 1171. After Nur al-Din's death, Salahuddin became the most famous of the Muslim anti-Crusader leaders. It was during this period that jihad literature was revitalized; for the first time in Islamic history, a truly broad-scale literature surfaced that praised jihad and those who engaged in it (Lawrence 2013: 134). The effect of such literature was to present jihad as a duty to preserve Muslim "territorial, political and symbolic integrity" (Lawrence 2013: 131).

Salahuddin captured Jerusalem in October 1187, thus fulfilling one of the major goals of the call to jihad. After Salahuddin's death in 1193, the remaining leaders of the Ayyubid dynasty lost focus on jihad, engaging instead in internecine conflict and making their own terms with the Franks (Hillenbrand 2000: 225; Ibn Athir 1995: 12:297). As such, Hulagu Khan and his Mongol forces were able to capture Baghdad on February 10, 1258, wreaking destruction to such an extent that it ended the golden age of Islam. According to Ibn Kathir (d. 1373), the Muslim historian and exegete, Hulagu's attacking 200,000 troops faced fewer than 10,000 demoralized and weakened defenders. Many of the Muslim soldiers had deserted their posts to be in the marketplaces or doorways of mosques (Ibn Kathir 2003: 13:202).

Salahuddin's Ayyubids were ousted by the Mamluks, who, under the leadership of Baybars (d. 1277) defeated the Mongols at Ain Jalut in 1260.

By the time of his death, Baybars had defeated most of the other claimants to leadership and established the Mamluk sultanate. In 1291, Sultan al-Ashraf Khalil (d. 1293) captured the city of Acre, thus effectively ending the Crusades. Almost two centuries of war against the Franks had resulted in a genre of jihad literature that focused on expelling the enemy as well as seeking to punish collaborators within the Muslim community. Ibn Taimiyyah (d. 1328), who lived during a time when the Mongols and Crusaders fought, as well as when Shia–Sunni politics played out, is arguably the most famous scholarly proponent of jihad in the thirteenth/fourteenth centuries. His emphasis on ridding the Muslim world of inimical outsiders and heretics was so powerful and far-reaching that even today, his writings are a main source of inspiration for extremists.

When the Ottomans later came to power, they used the jihad/*ghaza* ideology to encourage wars of empire building and to suppress their enemies within the Muslim community. Historians have questioned the religious nature of this jihad/*ghaza* ideology, especially since the Ottoman warriors often allied themselves with Christians and had non-Muslims in their ranks (Bonner 2006: 146; Bonney 2004: 128). As Cemal Kafadar has pointed out, *ghaza* meant raiding rather than a divinely mandated jihad (1995: 80). The Ottoman usage of jihad/*ghaza*, then, was distinct from the Islamic concept of a defensive war, and allowed for territorial expansion, booty, and glory (Kafadar 1995: 80). The Ottoman concept was therefore quite different from the jihad call of Saladin.

In 1435, Sultan Muhammad II defeated the Byzantines and conquered Constantinople, making it his capital city from which he made inroads into the Balkans. With the defeat of the Mamluks in Egypt, the Ottomans took over the office of the caliphate in 1517. By the middle of the sixteenth century, they became the most powerful empire in the world, controlling the Balkans, Jerusalem, Mecca, Medina, and much of Eastern Europe.

Under Ottoman rule, a massive bureaucratization brought about state control in every facet of religious life. Schools and colleges all fell under state control, and as such, Israeli Shlomo Goitein, one of the twentieth century's most distinguished scholars of Islamic studies, calls it the era of "Institutionalized Islam" (1968: 224–228). Nepotism, corruption, and bad governance plagued the Ottoman empire at the same time that European nations were reaping the benefits of the Industrial Revolution, developing weapons of war that would make the Ottoman machinery obsolete. On July 2, 1798, Napoleon Bonaparte's French forces landed in Alexandria, Egypt, and captured the city without a fight. Nineteen days later, in the Battle of the Pyramids, Napoleon routed the forces of the Ottoman commander, Murad Bey, killing some 5,000 of them while losing only 300 French soldiers. Modernity had forced home the fact that even with its jihad/ *ghaẓa* ideology, the Ottoman empire could not cope with the military and technological dominance of non-Muslim Europe. This started a period of colonization that was to affect Muslim populations everywhere.

The Second Call to Jihad: Pushback against European Influence and Colonization

By the beginning of the fifteenth century, three different empires – the Ottomans, Safavids, and Mughals – were in control of Muslim-majority areas. The most dominant of these, the Ottomans (Sunnis), held sway over Anatolia, Southeastern Europe, and nearly the entire Arab world, except for Morocco and certain areas in the Arab peninsula (Lawrence 2013: 135). The Safavids ruled Iran and parts of Turkey and Georgia. The Mughal empire, founded in 1526 by Babur, a descendant of the Mongol Timurlane, covered, at its zenith, Afghanistan, Baluchistan, and most of the Indian subcontinent. The scions of these dynasties all ended up fighting among themselves for power, descending into enjoying luxurious lifestyles that sapped the resources of their empires as the French and British became militarily stronger. By the end of the eighteenth century, all three empires were in tatters.

There were large Muslim communities in other places such as Senegambia, Sumatra, and the Caucasus, to name just three examples. These regions all experienced calls to jihad, with the Senegambian occurrence being the earliest. Like Mahmoud Mamdani, I count this as the second call to jihad. Unlike Mamdani, however, I list other areas as part of this call, since, while their involvement came later, they were certainly influenced by the initial success of the Senegambian revolt (Mamdani 2004: 50ff.).

The first African region to feel the effects of the Atlantic slave trade was Senegambia in the late fifteenth century. The European powers introduced firearms to the region, as they competed among themselves for dominance in the slave trade. The resultant socioeconomic and political upheavals in the area and the presence of firearms made for a terrible mix (Clarke 1982: 80). The Senegambian people were in a precarious position, caught between two sets of slave traders: Arab armies from the north, and the "expanding frontiers of the European slave trade in the south" (Mamdani 2004: 51). Led by local religious Sufi leaders (Marabouts), the Fulbe, the largest and most powerful Muslim group in the region, revolted in 1677. By 1690, they were victorious, and set up the imamate of Futa Jalon, dividing it into nine provinces. On the death of the last of the revolutionary leaders in 1751, however, the rule passed to military leaders who expanded their territory, in the process taking slaves from the non-Muslim communities against whom they waged war. The "jihad" that had started as a revolt against foreign influence and the slave trade ended up launching its own slave raids.

The Fulani jihad of Uthman dan Fodio (d. 1817), who founded the Sokoto caliphate, followed these series of wars. He rebelled against his Hausa overlords, and some have claimed that while he was a religious teacher, and labeled his movement a jihad, his movement was more about tribal supremacy than religious idealism (Gouilly 1952: 70; Meek 1925: 100). His son Muhammad Bello took a title hearkening back to the days of the earliest caliphate, appointing himself as "Commander of the Faithful." This movement also focused a lot on winning converts to Islam and creating a religious outlook that was rather puritanical (Bonner 2006: 152). A jihad, however, that was supposedly launched to promote a more egalitarian, ideal Islamic state resulted in the installation of a hierarchical polity with the Fulani trading and ruling classes as the prime benefactors (Keddie 1994: 463–487).

The jihads that occurred near to or during this time have certain common factors, echoing, as Nikki Keddie states, "parts of the original Islamic experience" (Keddie 1994: 463–487). They arose at a time when more powerful empires were on the decline and were situated close to those empires. In many of these regions, Islam was often the religion of the traders, and the early jihad warriors consisted primarily of traders, scholars, and nomads. In like manner, one finds that in Sumatra, the Padri Jihad movement was launched by traders. As noted earlier too, the jihads were often a response to economic, political, and cultural upheavals, not unlike the experience of the earliest Muslims.

In the early nineteenth century there was also a jihad movement in West Sumatra, also known as Minangkabau, located in western Indonesia. By the late eighteenth and early nineteenth centuries, the call for Islamic revival grew in the region based on arguments between the local village authorities. The region had been previously mined for gold, but with its depleted resources, and the increasing influence of European traders, new commodities were grown. The local communities started growing and exporting pepper, gambhir, cassia, and coffee. These commodities came from mountainous regions, and the transport caravans were subject to being waylaid and robbed. In 1803, a civil war started between the Padris, who wanted Islamic law enforced, and other groups. By 1820, the Padris controlled most of Minangkabau. The ousted ruling parties appealed to the Dutch, who attacked in 1821, but since they were engaged in a war in Java, signed a détente in 1825. After that war, however, the Dutch were able to concentrate their forces on the region, and in 1837 captured and exiled the Padri leader, Imam Bonjol. The jihad effectively ended.

The Third Call: The Wahhabi Jihad

In the middle of the eighteenth century, Muhammad ibn Abdul Wahhab (d. 1792) launched his jihad against the Ottomans, who, while Muslims, were outsiders in terms of ethnicity. While his summons was contemporaneous with other calls to jihad, I have listed it as separate given that it was in the heart of the homeland of Islam and directed primarily against coreligionists whom he deemed had committed either polytheism or heresy. He formed an alliance with a local Najdi chieftain, Muhammad ibn Saud (d. 1765). The major feature of this alliance was that Ibn Saud would fight against the enemy, while Abdul Wahhab would lead in religious affairs. They declared a war against *shirk* (polytheism). Their jihad movement culminated in the capture of Riyadh in 1773. These jihad warriors entered a strange agreement with the British in 1788: the British supplied them with arms in exchange for their assistance in the capture of Kuwait.

Abdul-Wahhab's success may be largely credited to the failure of the Ottoman state to grant him its full attention. In 1811, Muhammad Ali of Egypt defeated the first Saudi regime, which had embarked on a fanatical enterprise that saw an attack on the Shi'ite holy city of Karbala in 1802, and later, a murderous occupation of Mecca. The Saudis proved resilient, though, and came back to prominence in 1902, later forming an alliance with the Muslim Brotherhood movement (*Ikhwan*) in 1912. The combined forces imposed a strict form of Islam in the region that forced segregation of sexes, made communal prayers in mosques mandatory, and destroyed whatever buildings or relics that they felt encouraged deviation from strict monotheist worship. While the Ikhwan has largely disappeared, the modern Saudi regime had continued the alliance of the Houses of Saud and Abdul Wahhab. Oil revenues have catapulted Saudi Arabia to the leadership of the Muslim world, allowing for the financing of mosques and for imams in Muslim communities throughout the world to spread their particular version of Islam.

The Fourth Major Call: The Mahdist Revolt

In 1881, Muhammad Ahmed in the Sudan appointed himself the Mahdi and declared war against the British colonial administration. This had some unique elements to it from other jihad movements as it employed a messianic doctrine that relied on the non-Qur'anic apocalyptical traditions of the hadith literature. Using the imagery of early Islam, Muhammad Ahmed referred to his followers as "*Ansar*" (helpers); he deemed his flight from the British as a "*hijra*" and named those whom he had appointed to succeed him as "*khalifas*." This was a jihad against British colonization, as well as in opposition to the high taxation imposed upon the Sudanese people by the Ottoman Egyptian authorities (Mamdani 2004: 52). Initially, the Mahdi won several battles. In June 1882, his army of starving men, with spears and sticks, launched a dawn assault upon the army of Yusef Pasha, slaughtering all the Ottoman Egyptian forces. The spoils of this attack furnished him with an arsenal of guns and ammunition (Churchill 2004: 30). On January 25, 1885, the Mahdi captured Khartoum, but he died in the same month from typhus. His successor, Abdallahi ibn Muhammad, took over the rulership of the Mahdist state. His successors, apart from squabbling among themselves, tried to extend their territory and influence, waging their so-called jihad against neighboring countries, invading, among other places, Ethiopia. A war that started against occupation and oppression turned into a conflict that saw the Mahdist armies launching slave raids against their perceived enemies. In 1898, General Kitchener defeated the *khalifate* forces. To ensure that there were no further jihads, the British decided to make an example out of the Mahdi and destroyed his tomb, throwing his bones into the Nile.

There were numerous calls to jihad in the eighteenth and nineteenth centuries in various Muslim-majority areas, apart from those mentioned earlier in this Element. Most of them were associated with fighting against colonization. The leaders of the movements were generally very charismatic, often coming from Sufi backgrounds, such as dan Fodio, Imam Shamayl in the Caucasus, Imam Abd el-Qadir in Algeria, and Sayyid Ahmad Barelvi in India. Except for the jihads during the time of the Crusades, and that of Abd al-Wahhab in Saudi Arabia, the violence unleashed by these jihads, while initially directed against outsiders, ended up fomenting discord and disunity between the very peoples they were supposed to defend. The military and technological might of the European powers saw treaties of surrender for the most part being signed by the jihadists. While the call to jihad has always seemed a useful tool to motivate Muslim communities enough to fight against some perceived enemy, by the middle of the twentieth century, such summonses were largely ignored by the larger Muslim communities. In 1948, for example, as the Arab nations called for jihad against Israel, the other Muslim communities were content to sit as observers rather than fully commit warriors to the cause.

In 1967, in the face of the humiliating defeat that Israel inflicted upon the Arab nations, there was a conference at al-Azhar University, where a call to jihad was part of the results of the proceedings (Academy of Islamic Research 1970: 921–928). There was no global response on the part of the Muslim nations even though the jihad rhetoric was certainly present, and ideologues such as Abu Ala Maududi (d. 1979) and Sayyid Qutb (hanged in 1966) were calling for it. The jihadist ideology that their writings advocated was to come into play much later.

The Afghan Jihad

In December 1979, Soviet forces entered Afghanistan to support the pro-Soviet regime that had taken power in the country. That invasion cast Afghanistan as the main battlefield in a proxy war between the world's two superpowers: the United States and the USSR. The CIA and the Pakistani ISI banded together to support the Afghan *mujahideen* against the communist enemy. As Mamdani notes:

> Both intelligence agencies came to share a dual objective: militarily to provide maximum firepower to the mujahideen and, politically, to recruit the most radically anti-communist Islamists to counter Soviet forces. The combined result was to flood the region not only with all kinds of weapons but also with the most radical Islamist recruits. They flocked to ISI-run training camps in Pakistan, where they were "ideologically" charged with the spark of holy war and training in guerilla tactics, sabotage and bombings.
>
> (Mamdani 2004: 126)

Many Muslims from all over the world, energized by the 1979 Iranian revolution that overthrew the yoke of the United States in Iran, and now seeing the other superpower under attack, were mesmerized by the sudden turn of events. Volunteer warriors flocked to Afghanistan from places like Algeria, Saudi Arabia, Egypt, Indonesia, Sudan, Somalia, and other Muslim-majority countries. Some came from Europe and the United States. They included names that the world would come to dread: Muhammad Azzam and Osama bin Laden. Azzam was one of the founders of Hamas, but in 1980 could travel freely under the aegis of the CIA, rallying for support against the communist enemy.

For the first time in history, the United States supported a jihad movement, providing training and armament for modern guerilla warfare to the Afghan fighters. Several rival factions in Afghanistan formed a temporary alliance with the specific objective of expelling the Soviets. Osama bin Laden rose to prominence, as one of the leaders chosen by the United States (Mamdani 2004: 132). In 1989, the Soviets left Afghanistan, and America became the sole superpower with forces in the region. The *mujahideen* looked to continue their conflict, targeting larger objectives. The success of the Afghan jihad set in motion what Glenn Robinson of the University of California (Berkeley) terms "the four waves of global jihad" (Robinson 2017: 70–88).

While earlier jihad calls were specific to certain areas, the latest ones promote a global agenda. The ideologue behind the first wave of jihad was a Jordanian religious scholar, Abdullah al-Azzam (assassinated 1989). His ability to cite Qur'anic verses and hadith traditions to support his cause, along with his personal commitment, proved effective and he issued fatwas and writings that exhorted Muslims to retake the lands that had been lost to non-Muslim forces. For him, the two goals were Afghanistan and Palestine. Azzam, however, drew the line against fighting fellow Muslims, unlike other ideologues like Ayman al-Zawahiri, who wanted an all-out struggle against all perceived inimical entities, within and without the *umma*. Azzam was assassinated in 1989, with rumors flying that his death was brought about to still his opposition to the idea of fighting against fellow Muslims. He had argued for the formation of a base of well-trained warriors, "*al-Qaida*," and founded this organization in 1988 with the cooperation of many activists, including Osama bin Laden. The success of religiously inspired warriors against the mighty Soviets gave rise to the idea of waging jihad to liberate occupied Muslim lands all over the world, whether it be Palestine, Kashmir, Mindanao, or even Spain.

Shortly after the Russians exited Afghanistan, leaving hundreds of thousands of *mujahideen* with nothing to do except to engage in guerilla warfare, Iraq invaded Kuwait. Osama bin Laden proposed to the Saudi government that it send him to liberate Kuwait by using these trained warriors. After the government rejected his proposal and exiled him from Saudi Arabia in 1992, he shifted his base to Sudan.

In the first few years of this second wave of jihad, there were attacks in Somalia, in Tanzania, and on American ships in waters off the Arab peninsula. The infamous September 11, 2001 horror is the most important event in this wave. Osama bin Laden, while not a trained cleric, issued fatwas calling for *mujahideen* to take up arms against the United States, Israel, and any entity that he deemed threatened the survival of the Muslims. He had a certain charisma and, as the scion of an immensely wealthy family, access to billions of dollars. Many answered his call.

In Afghanistan, meanwhile, the Taliban rose to power, enforcing its own tribal concept of largely Pashtun tribal law (*Pukhtunwali*) under the guise of Sharia, and introducing an era of tyranny upon the citizens of the country (Ahmed 2003: 141). After 9/11, the United States declared war on Afghanistan and Osama bin Laden went on the run. In the meantime, several offshoot organizations in various parts of the globe, such as al-Shabab in Somalia, arose to use terrorism in their areas.

In 2003, the United States invaded Iraq and set into motion the third wave of global jihad. The Iraqi forces were routed, and it is from these that the manpower for the Islamic State in Iraq and Syria (ISIS) was created. Abu Musab al-Zarqawi formed Tawhid wa'l Jihad to fight against Shias. Muqtada al-Sadr established the Army of the Mahdi (*Jaysh al-Mahdi*) to fight against the American forces, but within a brief time, was pushed into simply trying to survive rather than form any effective resistance (Cochrane 2009). In 2010, Abu Bakr al-Baghdadi declared himself caliph of ISIS and set in motion a violence that caused mass displacement of refugees, with his men killing fellow Muslims,

Yazidis, Christians, and any individual who did not espouse his philosophy. In October 2017, the Syrian army claimed that Raqqa, capital of this new caliphate movement, was recaptured. There is still heavy fighting in the area, however, precipitating massive displacement of people along with civilian casualties that have resulted in the largest refugee crisis in modern times.

The fourth wave is the current stage of terrorism that seems likely to last for the foreseeable future, evidenced by the almost daily reports of atrocities. Whether it is Boko Haram, or bombings in Afghanistan or Somalia, there seems to be no joint effective policy of how to deal with the threat, especially as it has become outright terrorism and martyrdom operations. The Saudi war against Yemen, the Turkish operations against Kurds in Syria, as well as the crisis between Qatar and the rest of the Arab world, all indicate that violence in the Muslim-majority world will be there for the near term. Whether these are due to religion qua religion or to geopolitical issues couched in religious terms is of little importance since the main players are Muslims.

This fourth wave of jihad falls squarely into the Social Movement Theory (SMT) that scholars identify as one of the potential causes of religious violence, given the presence of the causative factors: political upheavals, organizations that can be mobilized to cause agitation, and narratives that justify violent actions (McAdam, McCarthy, and Zald: 1996). Akbar Ahmed notes that some Muslims have countered the process of globalization with the idea of a "post-honor" reaction (Ahmed 2003: 56). In this scenario, increasing global secularization and Western influence are seen as threatening the honor of Islam, and it is the duty of Muslims to defend the religion and its perceived values. Much of contemporary jihadist activism is not controlled by jurists who are genuinely steeped in Islamic learning, with any sense of ethics. Instead, movement leaders – the foremost example being Abu Bakr al-Baghdadi – selectively interpret scripture, abandoning all the classical Islamic protocols that see the lives of noncombatants as inviolable. By their charisma (see Weber 1991), leaders reinterpret scripture and relay fantastic images of reward, no matter how unreliable, to encourage their followers (see Tiersky 2016). Suicide operations are not part of the normative Islamic tradition and seem to be a strategy learned from the effectiveness of warfare strategies from outside groups, such as the Tamil Tigers (Pape 2005). The success of the early suicide missions from Hezbollah members has given rise to more daring attacks that now characterize some of the activities of the fourth wave of jihad.

To argue about the "true" meaning of the word in classical sources is to engage in an etymological fallacy, as the term is demonstrably used by terrorists in their terrorism. Underlining this scenario is the fact that many of today's violent jihadists are not from areas of conflict; rather they fall under the category of "homegrown terrorists" (Roy 2017). There is no standard profile of the terrorists, although the characteristics that abound show that they are often second generation, have a history of petty crime, are radicalized, are almost always "born again," and are able to use the latest gadgetry such as Twitter, Facebook, Whats App, etc. (Roy 2017). Their actions fit no standard operating procedure: the ramming of a vehicle into a crowd on Bastille Day, July 14, 2016 to slaughter eighty-four victims illustrates this new wave. The hostile rhetoric of many Western bloc nations, along with their efforts to bring about regime change in some Muslim-majority countries, only fosters the extremist mind-set that spawns more violence.

Islamic Law

Since 2010 more than 201 anti-Sharia laws have been introduced in forty-three states. In many cases, the framers of these bills admit that there is no actual threat of any Islamic law takeover, and that their motive is merely preventive. As some researchers have convincingly shown, the anti-Sharia scare is part and parcel of Islamophobia. Yet one cannot blame the masses of non-Muslims for being revolted by these depictions of Islamic law. Indeed, even Muslims themselves point out that what passes as "Islamic law" in many Muslim-majority countries is often tantamount to the most sanguinary savagery. Beheadings, honor killings, amputations, and public floggings come to mind easily when one reads of verdicts passed by *jirgas* and village magistrates, the pronouncements of ISIS, or the actions of village mobs in some places where people impose vigilante versions of Islamic law. In this section, I discuss the development of what we know as Islamic law, its descent into manifestations of physical violence, and the reasons for its problems.

The simple fact is that "Sharia law" is a misnomer. The word *sharia* is derived from the root that means "a path, a way." As used in Qur'an 5:48, "and for each amongst you, we have prescribed a path and a method," the term (and its derivatives) may be taken as similar in usage to when Jesus said, "I am the way, the truth and the life" (John 14:6). Here, Jesus does not define "way" – but the implication is obviously that he knows what it is. Since he does not explain it in detail, his followers must study his life and teachings carefully to decipher what it means to follow that way (path). As such, Professor Khalid Abou El-Fadl points out that "Shari'a is the eternal, immutable and unchanging law as it exists in the mind of God. Shari'a is the way of truth and justice as it exists in God's mind. In essence, Shari'a is the ideal law as it ought to be in the Divine realm, and as such it is by definition unknown to human beings on this earth" (Abou El-Fadl 2007: 150). No human therefore can claim to practice the Sharia: s/he can only hope to act in conformity with the ideals of Sharia.

The equivalent of a law school would be, in many Muslim-majority countries, termed "*Kulliyat al-Sharia*" – the Sharia College. What students learn there, however, is not "Sharia law," but legal theory and reasoning, known as *Usūl al-fiqh*. They use the fallible human intellectual reasoning, applying the process of understanding, which is known as *Fiqh*. What we refer to as Islamic law is actually "the fallible and imperfect attempt by Muslims over centuries to understand and implement the divine norms, to explore right and wrong, and to achieve human welfare ... importantly, what is called Islamic law is not contained in a single or few books. Islamic law is found in an enormous corpus of volumes that document the rulings, opinions, and discourses over the span of many centuries" (Abou El-Fadl 2014: xxxii). It covers a vast array of topics, from rulings related to worship, criminal law, personal status, family law, commercial law, international law, constitutional law, and inheritance. The Qur'an is not a legal text: only about 500 of its roughly 6,000 verses touch on what may be termed legislative topics; since many of those are more about ritual, or are repetitive, the truly legal verses of the Qur'an total only about eighty. The aspect of violence is more clearly manifested in criminal and apostasy laws; as such, I focus on these in this section, discussing the subject via a self-explanatory periodization schema.

Islamic Law during the Period of Revelation (610–632)

"ShaRa'A" – from whence comes *Sharia* – and its derivatives occur only five times in the Qur'an (Q 7:193, 5:48, 42:13, 21, and 45:18). In the single instance (Q45:18) where the word *sharia* is used, the direction is that Muhammad has to follow the "path" that is in relation to following what God has revealed, not only to him, but also to all the Prophets. During Muhammad's lifetime, there was no such thing as "Islamic law" as a corpus of rules and regulations. Since the Prophet saw himself as coming in the tradition of the Abrahamic prophets, his message was not meant to create an entirely new set of norms for the Arabian milieu to which the Qur'an was addressed. Rather, Islam's main document concerned itself with improving the standards governing the prevailing practices, and thus reformed but never completely replaced all of the patriarchal tribal values and customary laws of his time.

To be sure, there are verses of legislation in the Qur'an regarding theft, slander, brigandage, and sexual misconduct among other things, but there is considerable debate among the jurists as to what constitutes theft that warrants the amputation of a hand, or what exactly constitutes sexual misconduct (*zina*), since none of these crimes is defined legally in the Qur'an. In some cases there are clear punishments, while in others there is none, or there seems to be allowance for discretion regarding the imposition of such. Another fact that must be taken into consideration is that verses of legislation only came about after 622, when Muhammad fled the city of Mecca to relocate to Medina as leader of the first established community of believers. But several legislative aspects of the Qur'an indicate that:

> (W)hereas the spirit of the Qur'anic legislation exhibits an obvious direction toward the progressive embodiment of the fundamental human values of freedom and responsibility in fresh legislation, nevertheless, the actual legislation of the Qur'an has partly to accept the then existing society as a term of reference. This clearly means that the actual legislation of the Quran cannot have been meant to be literally eternal by the Quran itself.
>
> (Rahman 1979: 39)

Verses of gradual prohibition, such as in the case of intoxicants, indicate that, contrary to the general Muslim creedal position of decisiveness on any legal matter, the process of anything resembling legislation was a "slow, experimental tackling of problems" as they arose in the early community (Rahman 1979: 39).

Since Muhammad was the recipient of revelation, the decisions he rendered were not seen as coming from him, but from God. During the time of revelation, there was no understanding of a structured law as understood by later jurists, and Muhammad certainly left no code of laws. Apart from the tribal issues that were often decided by *hakams* (arbiters) as noted in the Qur'an (Q2:188, 4:35), God was seen as "the best of deciders" (*khayr al-fāsilīn*: Q6:57), ruling through Muhammad upon important matters that were either new or required divine guidance.

The Early Post-Prophetic Period (from 632 to circa 750)

Muhammad's unexpected death in 632 left the community without a divinely guided leader. I have put the end date of this period to coincide with the end of the Umayyad dynasty, as the records seem to indicate that, until this time, interpretations of the law were not done on a very structured basis. The recognition of a Muslim polity known as the caliphate, ruled by caliphs, represented a change from tribal government to one wherein humans, guided by the principles of Islam, were cast into leadership roles. These early communities, with the conquests and conversions, often faced issues in which there were no Qur'anic rulings. Initially, the caliphs themselves issued judgment. Outlying regions used *hakams* who interpreted the law to the best of their ability and who, without any structured magistracy, decided cases based on their own knowledge. Yet it seems clear that the caliphs exercised great latitude in interpreting verses of the Qur'an or enforcing law. Abu Bakr, the first caliph, for example, waged war against those who refused to pay the *ẓakat*, even though some of the other Companions were not in agreement on his decision (al-Alwani 2011: 43). Umar introduced the *diwan* – the register of those who received stipends in the caliphate (Coulson 1984: 23).

After the era of the first four caliphs, the Umayyad dynasty took over and its administrative method was to maintain law and order by relying on regulations already in place in many areas. This allowed for the importation of many distinctively foreign legal elements into the legal framework of the Islamic polity (Coulson 1984: 23). There is considerable debate as to when there was some sort of election of officials to a quasi-judiciary. Even though there are claims that Umar appointed Shurayh ibn Harith al-Kindi (died between 695 and 718) to be a *qāḍī* (judge), research shows that the earliest possible date for such an appointment would have been in 665, during the time of Muawiyah (Mohammed 2001: 191). As shown in Mohammed's doctoral dissertation on the subject, the attribution of Shurayh's appointment during Umar's caliphate was an attempt to assign the provenance of the personal rational interpretation (*ra'y*) to Umar. For later jurists of the Hanafi school of thought, Shurayh became the exemplar of the *sunna* in ninth-century Hanafi legal thought. Whatever the arguments on the subject, it seems clear that in the period when *qāḍīs* were first elected, there was no established set of protocols for issuing verdicts. By the end of the Umayyad period, however, the *qāḍīs* had evolved from being mere arbitrators in disputes, and customary laws were in some cases replaced by imported material from foreign systems, or from personal interpretations of applicable verses of the Qur'an. Still, however, a true code of legal thinking was not yet in place. As Coulson notes, "the task of the Umayyads had been to establish a practical system of legal administration, not a science of jurisprudence, and in this they had succeeded" (Coulson 1984: 35).

The Classical Period (800–1797)

It was under the Abbasid dynasty that the development of legal thought reached its zenith. I have arbitrarily chosen to give the end of that period as 1797, for no other reason than that year was the one in which Napoleon invaded Egypt, inaugurating the period of colonization. During this time, although the Qur'an was always the primary resource of the Muslims for their concept of divine guidance, the crystallization of the various sects and schools of thought came into being, with the major two recognized sects being the Shia and Sunni groups, each having certain differences in its approach to Islamic law.

This period saw the emergence of the various schools of thought that at one time numbered more than 100. By the tenth century, however, Sunni Islam knew four such schools: the Hanafi, Maliki, Shafi, and Hanbali. Among the

Shias, there were the Ja'fari and Zaydi schools. In general, the Muslim community accepted those differences, with each *madhab*'s opinion being valid for its followers. There is a special genre of literature for recording such differences known as *Ikhtilaf al-Fuqaha* – differences of the jurists – and this dates to quite early in Islam.[8]

---

[8] Several books bear this name. Perhaps the most famous classic is by Muhammad bin Jarir al-Tabari (d. 923), *Ikhtilā-f al-Fuqaha* (1980–1986). Ahmad al-Tahawi (d. 933) also published his own "Ikhtilaf al fuqaha" (1971). The reason for noting these authors is to show that quite early in Islamic history, jurists recognized that there was no one authority to issue Islamic legal verdicts. A narration in Ibn Sa'd (d. 845), the famous historian, makes the following claim about Imam Malik, the eponymic founder of the Maliki *madhab*:

> When Abu Ja'far [Caliph Mansur] performed Hajj, he called me. I went to see him and we talked. He asked questions and I replied. Then he said, "I have resolved to have several copies made of these books that you have composed. I will send one copy each to every Muslim city. I shall order the people to abide by its contents exclusively. I will make them set aside everything else than this new knowledge, because I find true knowledge in the tradition of Medina." I said, "O Commander of the faithful! Do not do that. Because the people have received various reports, heard several statements, and transmitted these accounts. Each community is acting upon the information they have received. They are practicing and dealing with others in their mutual differences accordingly. Dissuading the people from what they are practicing would put them to hardship. Leave the people alone with their practices. Let the people in each city choose for them what they prefer." Mansur said, "Upon my life! Had you complied with my wishes I would have ordered so."
>
> (Ibn Sa'd 1983: 440)

All these groups agree that the main sources of Islamic law are the Qur'an, the Sunnah, this being the practice of Muhammad and his Companions, and *Ijma* (consensus of scholars). Sunni Muslims claim the fourth source as syllogism, or *qiyas*, which is basically seeking to apply the ruling of one issue to another similar one based on some common factor between the two issues. Shias instead prefer to use the term *'aql* (intellect). The only difference between these two seems to be semantic as they both deal with assumption and the use of the fallible intellect.

Other sources are used for extrapolating legal opinions/rulings, but not all jurists agree upon their use. As such, Ibn Quddama (d. 1223), the Hanbali jurist, listed them in his work on legal theory under "*Usul mukhtalaf fiha*" – sources over which there is difference of opinion (al-Maqdisi 2003: 2:517). Among such sources are "*Shari'a man qablana*" – the laws of those before Islam (usually a reference to Jewish law), the opinions of Muhammad's Companions, *Istihsān* (juristic preference), *Istislāh* (public interest), and custom.

By applying interpretive methodologies to its verses and working with the Sunnah and the other sources of law mentioned in the foregoing paragraph, Muslim jurists formulated certain categories, such as Obligatory (*Fard/Wajib*), *Haram* (forbidden), *Mubah* (allowed), *Makruh* (Disliked), *Mustahab* (Preferred). The various methodologies applied by the jurists, however, made for a multiplicity of opinions. This period saw the formulation of the Fiqh Maxims, among which are axioms that are very similar to the Euro-American Law Maxims. Some examples are: "actions are by intention"; "custom has the weight of law"; "clarity is not superseded by doubt"; "necessity provides license," etc.

The idea of the Sunnah advanced along with certain developments that had not been previously elemental to majoritarian Islam. The jurists began to rely on the idea of *ijtihad*, intellectual reasoning, to reach decisions on matters that were new to them. They came up with clear ideas for testimony and processes by which to establish guilt of an accused. By a careful reading of the verses of the Qur'an and study of the hadith literature, they classified penalties into *hadd*, *ta'zir*, and *qisās*. *Hadd* is that punishment that the Qur'an (or hadith) clearly gives as the penalty for a particular offense (Coulson 1984: 124). As such, cutting off the hand of a thief is a *hadd* punishment, although there are conflicting opinions on the amount of the theft, or the manner in which it was committed to warrant such a penalty.

Another type of penalty is *ta'zir* – discretionary punishment, based on the opinion of the judge, either for crimes that are not specified, or for crimes that, while there may be a *hadd* penalty, do not reach the limit for the imposition of such, or where, for example, following the letter of the law would seem to allow for improper behavior. An example of such a case would be an unmarried couple caught in a compromising position short of sexual intercourse. Clearly, the couple cannot be punished for *zina*, but, according to Islamic norms, their conduct warrants some form of penalty. A judge in this case can order a discretionary punishment. The purpose of *ta'zir* punishment is generally seen as prevention of any conduct that is "prejudicial to the good order of the state" (Coulson 1984: 133).

Qisās is very similar to the Roman *lex talionis*, and eradicated the warfare that could ensue between tribes if someone were killed. In the pre-Islamic tribal system, the murder of a person could lead to long warfare between tribes, as often the tribe of a murdered person would demand the lives of several of the opposing tribespeople. Islam ameliorated this by making it a single life for a single life, and further allowed for the concept of forgiveness, with or without a blood payment (*dīya*).

Jurists also formulated what was known as the goals of the Sharia (*maqāsid al-sharia*), which were listed as protection of: (1) religion; (2) mind; (3) progeny; (4) human life; and (5) property. At some point, however, there was the idea that the doors of *ijtihad* (intellectual reasoning) were closed. As Wael Hallaq has pointed out, the concept is misunderstood, since intellectual juristic reasoning has never really stopped (Hallaq 1984). Yet originality for the most part had largely disappeared by the tenth century, and judicial developments generally occurred "within the framework of already established broader principles and methodology, rather than by radical innovation in either regard" (an-Na'im 2002: 7). Concomitant with this was the practice known as *taqlīd* wherein jurists were expected to impose the rulings of past cases upon present ones, since there was no room for independent thought.

Even though many Muslim scholars see the destruction of Baghdad in 1258 as the end of the golden age of Islamic thought, a malaise had set in by the end of the tenth century. Muslim thinkers had begun to deem the Qur'an as immutable and universal, the final revelation; that meant its injunctions were applicable to every society, in every place and time, even though the Qur'an itself does not make this claim.

After the destruction of Baghdad in 1258, the Muslim polity went into a steep decline. The Mamluks installed a caliphate in Egypt, but were defeated in 1517 by the Ottomans, who took the office of the caliphate to Istanbul. The time between the fall of Baghdad and Napoleon's invasion of Egypt in 1797 marks a most distinct phase in the periodization of Islamic history. This period was noted for the dominance of non-Arab Mamluks and Ottomans over the Islamic world. There was massive bureaucratization and the state ended up controlling every facet of life. Shlomo Goitein notes of this period that "religious creativity was largely replaced by obscurantism and true ecstatic mysticism by speculative theosophy" (Goitein 1968: 224–228). Yet, despite the general malaise, throughout the Islamic polities, state or privately funded seminaries provided rigorous training in Islamic legal thinking. If the general feeling was that Islamic legal thought had become ossified under the supposed closure of the doors of *ijtihad*, there was general regard for a plurality of opinions on any given subject. The governments still therefore relied on jurists to provide rulings on what was permissible or prohibited within the religion.

The Period of Colonization (1797–1950)

I have chosen the end of this time frame to represent the general period when the former colonies were being granted independence. The general narrative is that the colonizers occupied Muslim-majority lands and replaced the existing Islamic laws with European ones (al-Shafie 2003: 1–12). While this is true for the most part, the fact is that the colonizers were never fully successful in replacing Muslim laws, and as such, a weird mix occurred: the colonizers had to make room for the laws of the occupied lands in the judicial systems that they administered. They could not, for example, completely erase the system of polygyny. Even in places with non-Muslim majorities, such as the British territories in the Caribbean (for example, British Guiana and Trinidad), special accommodations were made for Muslims who wished to engage in polygyny.

The colonial legal systems had to accommodate what was known as Muhammadan Law. Under colonial rule, British legal professionals received training in this "Muhammadan Law," and in India, for example, the British-installed judges had to employ Muslim legal experts as consultants (Moosa 2009: 159). The colonial idea was that the colonies had to be saved from their native backwardness and systems by making compromises when necessary to prevent descent into total chaos. Dutch Orientalist Snouck Hurgronje wrote in the most dismissive terms of Islam and its constructs: "The treasuries of Islam are excessively full of rubbish that has become entirely useless; and for nine or ten centuries they have not been submitted to a revision deserving that name" (Hurgronje 1916: 139).

While various Muslim-majority countries may have had differences in the way the colonialists tried to wreck the edifice of centuries of Islamic legal practice, the examples of what happened in India in particular reflect the general approach. In India, Warren Hastings, the first governor of Bengal and head of the Supreme Council (from 1772 to 1785), wrote that Islamic criminal law was "a barbarous construction, and contrary to the first principle of civil society" (Moosa 2009: 165).

He replaced Islamic criminal law and imposed British criminal law. In doing so, he exchanged a communitarian approach with a system that focused on the individual, paying little attention to the community. This method was used by administrators of the colonial system to regard local Islamic legal systems as irredeemably barbaric. While, as noted earlier, some laws were incorporated into the system, the general framework of Islamic law was reduced to local folk or customary practices. Unlike Islamic law, in the case of murder for example, where family members could claim justice, the colonial system made these relatives mere witnesses to the judicial process (Moosa 2009: 167). The *dīya* that was used as material compensation in the Islamic system became illegal.

The result was that Islamic law was relegated to the status of customary law, and even Muslims who gained positions in the judiciary were trained primarily as secular professionals in Western-styled law schools. The institutions or *awqāf* (endowments) that had previously financed Sharia students were closed. The famous institutions of Islamic learning, such as al-Azhar in Cairo, became state institutions. The graduates were no longer respected as were their predecessors; instead they became civil servants acting upon the orders of the state. The role of the *ulama* was reduced to leading prayers or, at best, serving as judges in personal law courts (Abou El-Fadl 2007: 37). The curricula of these institutions were severely curtailed and instead of being trained in the finer points of Islamic law, students were trained to be basically chaplains, powerless religious functionaries who could not truly influence social or political policy.

In many Muslim lands, reformers such as Jamal al-Din Al-Afghani, Muhammad Iqbal, Muhammad al-Shawkani, Rifa'i, al-Tahtawi, Rashi Rida, etc. tried to call for a reform in Islamic thought, showing that Islamic constructs were completely compatible with modernity. It is difficult to estimate the impact of their attempts, as noted by Khalid Abou El-Fadl, since the political developments of their times often marginalized their efforts (Abou El-Fadl 2007: 37).

The Postcolonial Period (1950 to the Present)

The current state of Islamic law in every single Muslim-majority nation seems to be that of outright confusion. Saudi Arabia lingers under a literalist interpretation of medieval law that still enacts the amputation of hands for thieves, the flogging of those accused of public drunkenness, and the stoning of adulterers. In Pakistan, Indonesia, Sudan, Iran, and Yemen, Islamic law seems to be enacted without any reference to the goals of the Sharia to promote what would seem to be ethical and moral practices to please the Divine. Many would-be reformers call for an innovative approach that would promote some sort of merciful interpretation of the law, but in the modern world of the nation-state, it seems impossible to introduce any system of Islamic law that is based on a humane approach. The general interpretation of Islamic law seems to be to try to work on the idea of the permanency of the details of medieval interpretations. It seems inevitable that the Muslim-majority states will rely more on Western approaches to law or reinterpret the goals of the Sharia to provide license for the import of modern Western laws under the veneer of reform.

Apostasy

Within the past two decades, discussions and impositions of the death penalty for apostasy and same-sex relations have become prevalent. Some more conservative elements hold that a Muslim cannot renounce Islam and that scripture and tradition prohibit same-sex relations. Modern scholars who study classical Islamic law treatises about apostasy often read these texts without consideration of the presumed situation those texts address. As such, they assume that any utterance or action by a Muslim that is deemed heretical or as clear evidence of renunciation of the Islamic faith warrants the death penalty. The problem with this assumption is that while the Qur'an condemns apostasy, insofar as apostasy simply means renouncing Islam, it does not prescribe any punishment for it (as is evidenced in verses Q2:217, 4:90, 5:54, 5, 16:108, and 47:25. The Qur'anic verses indicate that one is free to accept or leave Islam since "there is no compulsion in religion" (Q2:256). The punishment, if any, will be in the life to come, as in Q4:137 that states: "Those who believed, then disbelieved, then believed, and then disbelieved [once more] and became more committed to disbelief, God will not forgive them or guide them to the righteous path" (an-Na'im: 2013).[9]

The Arabic word for apostasy is *ridda*, which means to "turn back." As discussed in the section on jihad, however, it has to be understood that it is not the mere denial of Islam that led to war against the Quraysh, but rather that they sought to kill the Muslims. During the classical period, Muslim jurists wrote according to the practices of their time. Their division of the world into *Dar al-Islam* and *Dar al-Kufr* meant that, for all intents and purposes, Muslims and non-Muslims were deemed to be in a state of perpetual

[9] Here I am using the translation of Professor Abdullahi an-Na'im with a very minor change, rendering his "pathway" as "path." See "Islam and the Secular State: Rethinking Apostasy and Shari'a" (an-Na'im 2013).

hostility towards each other (Abou El-Fadl 2007: 225). A vast number of jurists at that time, writing when the Islamic polity was at the zenith of its power, felt that any non-Muslim nation was hostile unless a specific treaty dictated otherwise. This corresponds to medieval Christendom's view of non-Christian states. In broad terms, there was a power struggle between Christendom and Islamdom for the sovereignty of the universe. In such a situation, a resident within the Islamic polity who renounced Islam was denying his fealty to the Islamic state and identifying himself as an enemy. This is not unlike the way an American would be viewed if he were to publicly reject his citizenship and declare allegiance to al-Qaeda. Today, in many Muslim-majority states, authorities use blasphemy and apostasy laws to control and coerce non-Muslim minorities, or to prevent any sort of dissent from prevailing interpretations of Islam, as is evident in the treatment of the Ahmadi Muslims in Pakistan.

Same-Sex Relations

On June 26, 2015, the US Supreme Court issued a landmark verdict in the *Obergefell* v. *Hodges* case, ruling that, per the due process and equal protection clauses of the Fourteenth Amendment to the US Constitution, all fifty states had to perform and recognize same-sex marriages. By comparison, on a global scale, many of the countries that prescribe a death sentence for same-sex relations are Muslim-majority states. Some states do differentiate between the treatment of male–male relations and female–female relations; in the latter case, the death penalty is not on the books (Bearak and Cameron 2016).

A survey of Muslims after the *Obergefell* ruling showed confusion on the issue among people in general regarding such relations: in general terms, about 50% of Muslims and Christians were against same-sex marriage (Shackford 2016). This is to be expected since the followers of the Abrahamic religions generally use the same source narrative (i.e., the

Sodom and Gomorrah story), with the same extrapolations to justify an anti-LGBTQ position. This was not surprising, given the interpretations given to the Qur'anic narrative about Sodom and Gomorrah, as well as Qur'an 4:16, which refer to punishing the two parties in same-sex intercourse (although such punishment seems left to the discretion of the authorities), as well as the hadith narratives on the matter. Dr. Jasser Auda, regarded by many Muslims as representing a modern intellectual, confessional approach to Islamic law, issued a rather surprising condemnation of the ruling. In summary, he pontificated that while the Supreme Court decision permitted same-sex marriages, this fact did not change its status within Islamic law, and that the Islamic position can never change (Auda 2015).

Even more strangely, Dr. Auda admitted that evidence indicates that the Prophet himself, as well as his Companions, had treated people of mixed gender with dignity (see Rowson 1991: 671–693). He also pointed out that, in Islam, "no orientation is a 'sin' per se, and all forms of sexual desires are tests from God in this worldly life. However acting upon one's desire is a totally different matter." He goes on to state that "two males or two females cannot possibly get married under the Islamic law. These provisions are an integral part of Islam and are not subject to alternative interpretation or any difference of opinion among scholars of Islamic law. The purpose for this prohibition has been clearly and extensively researched by such scholars in light of the sanctity of marriage as divinely ordained and its purposes and higher objectives."

There are several problems with Auda's assumptions. He never seems to ask why God would create a group of people with an orientation that in itself was not sinful, but then deny those people the right to act based on what the Divine created them with. He seems to place what passes as Islamic law under some nimbus of sanctity when scholars of Islam, without any exception known to me, admit that Islamic law, or *Fiqh*, is a fallible human enterprise. Auda seems to completely overlook what is accepted fact in general academic theory:

namely, that our concepts of sexuality of previous eras are skewed by our use of terms such as *homosexuality*, and that our perceptions are skewed by our own heteronormative understandings based on interpretations of biblical and qur'anic texts.

Several scholars, however, such as Scott Kugle, Amina Wadud, and Everett Rowland, have researched the history of sexuality in Islamicate societies and come to different conclusions than Jasser Auda. Their findings correspond to As'ad Abu Khalil's:

> In writing about the subject, a distinction should be made between attitudes towards homosexuality – and indeed towards sexuality in general – in Arab/Islamic history, and the prevalent attitude towards sexuality in some contemporary Arab societies. In the past, Muslims (from the time of Muhammad onwards) talked about sexuality without inhibitions or moral restraints. We learn from the writings of Al-Jahiz, for example, that Muslim men and women talked explicitly about sexual matters in mosques and during the Hajj, which is something inconceivable today ... Among the Sunni theologians, Imam Malik permitted heterosexual anal intercourse in his *Kitab As-Sirr*.
>
> (Abu Khalil 1993: 32–34, 48)

One medieval belletrist, al-Jahiz (d. 868/9 CE), wrote a book, *Mufakharat al Jawari wa'l Ghilman* (*Virtues of Women and Young Boys*), referring here to the enjoyment of sexual relations with them (al-Jahiz 1957). Another book is the more famous *Al-Rawd al-'Atir fi Nuzhat al-Khātir* of Muhammad al-Nafzawi (d. 1324 CE), rendered into English by Richard Burton as *The Perfumed Garden* (al-Nafzawi 1963). Indeed, medieval Christian writers assailed Islam for its perceived laxity and permissiveness in sexual matters (Djait 1978), disparaging the Qur'an for its imagery of a heaven in which there is mention of "houris and ghilman" (as in Q52:24, 55:70, 56:17, 76:19).

While some texts refer to same-sex relations by the term *Liwāt* (extracted from the term meaning "the people of Lot"), the majority opinion seems to obfuscate that the relevant Qur'anic verses clearly refer to rape rather than consensual sex. The Qur'an is not concerned with the historicity of the event depicted, but with what lessons it holds for Muslims. It has Lot ask his people, "do you approach men instead of women, out of lust?" (Q: 7:81). The qualifier "out of lust" here shows that the reason was not innate, but that it was out of choice. The narrative reveals too that this was not a matter of consent, for Lot was being commanded to produce his guests for the rabble, regardless of what the guests wanted. This would mean that same-sex rape was the objective. What the Qur'an was speaking about, then, was a clear case that had little to do with sexual orientation, or relations based on love, mutual respect, and consent. Andalusian Ibn Hazm, even as a man of his time, stated that the reason for punishment was based not only on their sexual activity, but on their having rejected divine guidance (Adang 2003: 5–31).

Scott Kugle has written extensively about the Qur'anic directives, astutely focusing on a verse that faith adherents might see as a reference to the modern finding of psychological programming (Kugle 2007: 131–168; 2010: 47; for a supporting viewpoint, see also Jahangir and Abdul Latif 2015: 198, 226). Q17:84, states: "Each one acts upon 'shākilatihī.'" The word comes from the verb that means "to shape." In a modern context, it may be inferred that this is God given, and therefore the issue of choice is completely out of the question. On the issue of sexual relations, the Qur'an, in its heteronormative mode, does not deal with what today we may term "gay" relations. While Qur'an 4:16 seems to specifically target sodomy, then, given the prevalence of literature and Muhammad's own actions indicating harmonious interaction with "the *mukha-natheen*," one may gather that Arab society, not unlike that of Paul's of the

Christian testament, was more concerned with perceived gender roles. Private matters were one thing, but actions that four people witnessed were against the public concept of propriety.

The neo-fundamentalist approach in many Muslim-majority nations comes with horrible consequences for gays, lesbians, bisexuals, transgender, and those who are questioning their sexual identity. In a total switch from medieval perceptions, a draconian approach has largely replaced the liberal attitude in many Muslim-majority states. Even the accusation of related impropriety in cases can lead to death, and in Malaysia, the conviction of Anwar Ibrahim, a former deputy prime minister, definitely destroyed his hopes of becoming prime minister. Despite this situation, Islamicate societies have long known overt same-sex relationships, and associations that fight for same-sex rights are present in many places. Some organizations are registered in countries where they can conduct their activities without fear and have a large social media presence, such as, for example, al-Fatiha (United States), Salaam Canada, and the Safra Project (United Kingdom). Others work in fear of reprisal and as such, try to avoid publicity (al-Bedaya in Egypt, for example). The Inner Circle of South Africa, a group that since 2003 has been sponsoring annual conferences on same-sex relations, is the world's largest Muslim LGBTQ organization. The leader of the community, Imam Muhsin Hendricks, trained in Pakistan, took advantage of South Africa being one of the first countries to outlaw discrimination based on sexual preference. While the bulk of the participants are of the LGBTQ community, many straight scholars are invited to provide their input, and in recent years, the *mufti* of Zambia, Shaykh Assadullah Mwale, has been a very strong advocate of recognizing that sexual orientation is not a matter of choice. Even without such conferences and organizations, however, LGBTQ activism continues in Muslim-majority countries. In the May 2007 issue of *The Atlantic*, Nadya

Labi reported that, despite the official forbiddance of such relations, Riyadh was deemed "a gay heaven" by one of the interviewees (Labi 2007).

Conclusion

In the modern era, many majority-Muslim states, in an effort to replace the impact of colonialism, or the perceived influence of the Western bloc countries, have resorted to seeking solace in some idealized past of law and order. Under the influence of rigid interpretations of Islam from Sudan, Saudi Arabia, and Pakistan, the manifestations of violence are becoming clearer.

The imposition of Sharia on the non-Muslim south of Sudan was a key factor in the civil war that started in 1983 and ended in 2005. More than two million Sudanese died in this conflict that ended with the secession of South Sudan in 2011. The government in Sudan executed Mahmoud Taha, an influential thinker, in 1985 for daring to call for an end to such an interpretation and imposition of Sharia. A similar situation exists in many of the other Muslim-majority states.

In 1977, General Zia-ul-Haqq, as part of his Islamization process, introduced what he called the "*hudood* law" to replace parts of the Pakistan penal code dating from the British era. The *hudood* law lists the categorizations of *hudood*, *ta'zir*, and *qisās* that include punishments for blasphemy and intoxication. Particularly problematic are the sex-related offenses of adultery and premarital intercourse. Cases of rape are especially troublesome since the Pakistani jurists seem to have confused adultery and rape. In the former, four witnesses must bear testimony. In the case of rape, nothing in the hadith or Qur'an indicates the requirement of witnesses; in Pakistan, however, the jurists required the same for rape. Considering that often rape is not committed in front of witnesses, it is difficult for a woman to obtain a conviction. More egregiously, if she gets pregnant, she can be charged for adultery or fornication. If she does not become pregnant, and still cannot provide witnesses to the crime, she may be guilty of *qadhf* – making a false accusation – and be whipped in public for this. These laws, rather than manifest the establishment of any utopian state, simply harass and persecute people. A survey by Charles Kennedy of the University of Michigan indicated that these laws mainly affect the poorer segment of the populace, as 2% of convictions were among the middle class, and absolutely none among the upper class (Kennedy 1996: 77). A survey of the sexual misconduct laws, for example, showed three common patterns:

1. A man and a woman are accused of *zina* by the father or older brother of the accused woman, the complainant(s) not consenting to the marriage or relationship;
2. A complainant accuses his "former" spouse of *zina* when she remarries;
3. A girl could bring charges of rape against her "boyfriend" if her relatives confront her with alleged evidence of possible wrongdoing or dishonor.
      (Kennedy 1996: 56–58)

In Saudi Arabia, a similar system is in place, with punishments often performed on Fridays after the congregation prayer in public squares. I have personally witnessed beheadings of those found guilty of drug peddling. There have been cases of stoning for adulterers and amputation of the hands of convicted thieves. This overt physical violence is only one aspect of the negative effect of such an interpretation of Islamic legal thought. I have not seen any detailed studies of the psychological, economic, or other societal effects on those so punished. It is clear, however, that accused persons being placed in jail or whipped for drunkenness, or migrant workers being sent home for violation of laws (without their wages being paid to them) all have disastrous consequences.

The battle for Islam, as Khalid Abou El-Fadl notes, is between moderates and those he deems "puritans," based on their vision of a pure

Islam if certain laws and practices are enforced (Abou El-Fadl 2007: 162). Entities like ISIS and Boko Haram, in their effort to fight the Western forces, are imposing their own brand of Islamic law that has little to do with methodology or consideration of the goals of the Sharia, as understood by the classical jurists. Such "puritans" view most modern Muslims as having strayed from the path of righteousness and in need of coercion to return to what is proper. Many of the proponents for "Islamization of law" are not scholars in the field, and as such, bring about what Scott Appleby (2002: 85–92) and Khalid Abou El-Fadl (2014: 119) term the "vulgarization" of Islamic law. This means a return to an imagined, highly artificial Islam that draws a clear line of demarcation between an ungodly Western "them" and a righteous "us." The actors in this scenario seek to gain their goals without any of the ethical or moral considerations elemental to the Islamic tradition, employing instead the cruelest methods to achieve their ends. A good example is the *hudood* ordinance of Pakistan.

Moderates do call for a reform in Islamic law via the return to considering *"maqasid al-sharia."* This is exercising law with objectives in mind rather than usually classical precedents. These objectives are: the preservation of human life, the preservation of the faculty of human reason, the preservation of the freedom of religion, the preservation of honor, and the preservation of material wealth (Attia 2007: xii). These jurists and thinkers, however, are part of the intellectual elite, and their words have little effect on the governmental ideas of Islamization. I do not see any possibility of momentous reform, since such processes take a long time. Muslims, in general, see themselves as a beleaguered community. In such circumstances, there is more of a desire to circle the wagons and rely on the glory of an imagined past rather than to engage in critical reflection with the possibility for reform.

Patriarchy As Violence

The Qur'an did not create an entirely new set of norms for the Arabian milieu to which it was initially addressed. Rather, Islam's main document concerned itself with improving the standards governing the prevailing practices, and thus reformed but never completely replaced the Arabian patriarchal tribal values and customary laws. As such, the Qur'an may be seen as a cultural document in that it was aimed at a particular people in light of their tribal traditions and worldview.

Like the antecedent scriptures of the Abrahamic faiths, the Qur'anic verses clearly endorse patriarchy as a norm. While many Muslims may hold that the actual legislation of the Qur'an was never meant to be permanent, and that the document ought to be a guide for the progressive embodiment of egalitarianism and freedom from oppression, the fact is that normative understandings of that document endorse patriarchy (Barlas 2002: 22; Rahman 1979: 79). Since it is the foundation of Islamic understanding, its exegeses, as well as the hadith literature and the understanding of Islamic law, make the patriarchy seem sanctioned and ordained by God, who uses the masculine pronoun in self-reference.

To ensure the institutional understanding of the patriarchy as a divine imposition, the senior scholars of Saudi Arabia, at an all-male conference in Taif in 1995, responded to the statement of resolutions of the United Nations-sponsored Fourth World Conference on Women (held in Beijing from September 4–15, 1995) thus:

> The goal of this document[10] is to wantonly unbridle one's desires, to allow that which is far from any morality, to remove people from the natural state in which God has created them. It is known

---

[10] I.e., the statement of resolutions of the conference.

that the Muslim woman does not face problems insofar as her status in society is concerned, for she is a mother, a wife, a sister and a daughter. The Sharia of Islam has accorded her all rights, with preservation from vulgarity and debasement in every aspect of honor/dignity and respect, and given her rights, all of which are appropriate to her constitution that her Creator has given her ... And the men have been preferred above them in many rulings, such as inheritance, testimony and other issues.

(al-Juraysi 2007: 1838)

The document concluded:

Because of the foregoing, the committee of higher scholars of Saudi Arabia calls upon Muslims: governments, nations, scholars, organizations, societies, and individuals to condemn the program of the (women's) conference. They must warn against it and invite all to rebut the goals that we have already outlined, and to reject what God and his Prophet have rejected. They must do this to protect Muslims from falling into such conduct. God is the authority over us, the One who grants success.

(al-Juraysi 2007: 1838)

Herein lies the problem for Muslims. The *weltanschauung* thus endorsed as a divine mandate is not just about the rule of men. It endorses the inextricable connection between religion, violence, and patriarchy, and infantilizes women (Rakozcy 2004: 30). The general status of Muslim women in almost every aspect of Islamic law places them as victims according to the definition of violence as "the attempt of an individual or group to impose its will on others through any nonverbal, verbal or physical means that will inflict psychological or physical injury" (Nessan 1998: 451). Among the most obvious cases are those of marriage, inheritance, testimony, sex and spousal violence, clothing, dowers, education, employment, freedom of travel, leadership, and honor killings.

Male dominance in the Qur'an is evidenced in the use of nomenclature that denotes a patrilineal system. Qur'an 33:5 states, "call them by [the names] of their fathers." In the society of Muhammad, the male oversaw providing for the family, and it was for this reason that the Qur'an made him the protector and manager of his wife's affairs: "Men are the protectors and maintainers of women because of that which God has favored one above the other, and because they support them from their means" (Qur'an 4:34). It is also because of this that sons receive twice as much as daughters in inheritance, and the two-to-one ratio applies to male beneficiaries over their female counterparts in general (Qur'an 4:11).

Another case of nomenclature indicating male superiority is in the divorce verse, Q2:228, where the Qur'an uses *bu'ool* (singular *ba'l*) in reference to husbands. This word, unlike *zawj* (one of a pair), connotes manifest superiority (compare Q2:228 with Q37:12); this was the term used for a false god, as well as to indicate the elevated status of a husband (Q2:228; see "Ba'al and Ba'al-Worship," Jastrow, McCurdy, and McDonald in *Jewish Encyclopedia*, 1906). The end of that verse (Q2:228) also notes, "the men are a degree above them (wives)," thus leaving little doubt regarding the gender hierarchy.

The Qur'an generally refers to females in terms of their relationship to a male, rather than by their own name. As such, we see references to "the wife of Lot" and "the wife of Noah." Mary, mother of Jesus, is the only woman mentioned by name in the Qur'an. While many Muslims point out that this is a position of great honor, and that she is hailed as the purest of women (Q3: 42–43), her superiority over the other members of her gender is because of her purity and chastity – values that are cherished for a woman in patriarchal society.

The woman's role as mother and housekeeper has made it difficult for the general body of exegetes to accept that women could be prophets, since such an office would mean interaction with the society at large, an image seemingly at odds with the Arab tribal concept. The Qur'an does not even hint at female prophets, and many use Q21:7 to insist on maleness as a prerequisite for prophethood, since the verse states, "We did not before you except men to whom We gave revelation."

In the relevant verses about the fall of the primordial couple from divine grace, God pointedly only addresses Adam and never mentions the spouse's name. Q2:35 narrates God's direction to the couple, wherein the Divine addresses the man. "You and your wife may reside in the garden and eat plentifully of whatever you wish, but do not come near to this tree for then you will be among the wrongdoers." The Muslim tradition renders her name as Hawaa (Eve), the Arabic equivalent of the Hebrew Hava (Eve), sourced from the Hebrew Bible via the hadith.

The coming of Islam to the Arab peninsula lifted wives from their former status as chattels, and made them instead partners in whom husbands could find tranquility and completeness. The Qur'anic verse illustrates this change of position:

> And among His signs is that He created for you mates from among yourselves that you may dwell in tranquility with them. And He has put love and mercy between you. Verily, in that, are signs for those who reflect!
> (Q30:21)

In line with this verse, the Qur'an specifies that a woman has rights as well as obligations and that a husband should not force her to live with him to maltreat her (Q2:228, 231). Instead of the limitless polygyny of pre-Islamic Arabia, the number of wives a man may have is limited to four, although this is ideally contingent on fair treatment (Q4:3). It ought not to be overlooked, however, that the Qur'anic language indicates that the authority for marriage lies with males, and that women must seek the permission of their male guardians for marriage (Q2:221).[11] Indeed, the tradition in some Muslim-majority countries does not even require the bride's verbal assent to her marriage: a male guardian speaks on her behalf. A hadith report buttresses this practice, stating that the bride's express consent is not needed for a marriage: her acquiescence is denoted by her quietness (Ibn al-Hajjaj 1992: 2:714). When it comes to interfaith marriage, Qur'an 5:3 clearly states that marriage to "women of the people of the book" is permitted. Without getting into the issue of what "people of the book" exactly means, the majoritarian interpretation is that only Muslim males may marry women who are not Muslim (Mohammed 2017: 374). The husband is the leader of the home and the children follow his religion. Few imams will perform a marriage ceremony between a Muslim woman and a non-Muslim man, as they fear that any children of that marriage will be non-Muslims. In cases where a Muslim woman goes against her family's wishes and does enter such a marriage, she often faces ostracism, and in some cases, may even be subject to the threat of honor killings. This patriarchal interpretation comes with further issues too: for many conservative preachers, the "people of the book" is an exclusive term for Jews and Christians. In this worldview, Muslim men may not marry Hindus, Buddhists, Jains, or women from any other religions.

---

[11] See, for example, Abu Da'ud al-Sijistani, *Sunan Abi Dawud* (1996) 2:95: "The Prophet said three times, "For any woman who marries without the permission of her guardians, her marriage is null and void. If the marriage is consummated, then the dower is for her because of what she has undergone; and if they dispute, then Satan is the guardian of the person who has no guardian.""

There are specific rules in the Qur'an, hadith, and Islamic legal treatises regarding divorce. While the scripture certainly seems to amend certain conditions in which women were horribly treated, the improvements were only in relation to the seventh-century conditions of Muhammad's milieu. The scriptural direction does not give the woman the right to initiate divorce, but rather instructs the husband on the process. This involves a period of trying to make things work, and ideally, the divorce stretches over the time for three menstrual periods. The idea is that at the end of each, the husband makes an utterance of divorce after careful contemplation about the effects of such a pronouncement. If after the end of three periods, three utterances are made, then the divorce is deemed final and irrevocable (Q2:228). It is a widely known practice, however, for men to utter three pronouncements at one time, and thus end the marriage.

The hadith literature and Islamic law do allow for a woman to be the petitioner for a divorce via a process known as *khul'* (Mohammed 2017: 368). This is based on a hadith reported in all the major tradition collections, wherein the wife of one of the Prophet's Companions stated that she could no longer stand her husband.[12] The Prophet asked her if she would return the dower of an orchard of date palms. When she assented, he granted the divorce and decreed that her period of *idda* (abstention before contracting another marriage) to be a single menstrual cycle. Two things stand out in this reported case: the first is that the woman is not really in charge of the divorce: a judge has to rule on its validity. The second is that she had to return the dower. Since the dower is essentially the price paid for the rights to her sexuality, and if she has to return that, then it means that she has surrendered her sexuality for nothing, i.e. that

---

[12] There are several versions of the hadith with varying explanations for her wanting the divorce. Some say that the husband was extremely ugly; others claim he was impotent.

the husband has enjoyed the right to her physical and sexual being and is being compensated for leaving the marriage (see Ali 2013: 4).

Since the Qur'anic directives are to a male audience and mirror the reality of a seventh-century environment, some of the Qur'an's counsel on the solution of marital discord has been the subject of vehement contemporary debate. Qur'an 4:34 advises that a good wife is obedient to God and guards her chastity in her husband's absence. The verse goes on to instruct the husbands who fear *nushūz* (often explained as rebellion against the husband's authority) from their wives that they should first admonish them, and then ostracize them in the bedroom (Ali 2013: 120–121). If the situation does not get better, the husbands may then resort to physical punishment. Instead of focusing on the idea that the verse was addressed to a society in which wife-beating seems to have been a norm, and that antecedent scriptures never saw such as a problem, traditional exegetes have seen the verse simply as a prescription of the rights of the husband over his wife's person. It is true that most have relied on hadith to explain that a beating should not draw blood or break the skin. Such interpretations, however, do not seem to consider that injuries are not limited to being physical, and that regardless of what method is used to discipline an adult, it is still abuse. As Ayesha Chaudry has noted in her conclusion on the study of this verse, "a patriarchal idealized cosmology reigned supreme in the pre-colonial period, which justified the moral and disciplinary oversight of husbands over wives and sanctioned husbands to use physical discipline when necessary" (Chaudry 2013: 22). Today, while an abundance of literature raises ethical objections to such dominance over wives, the majoritarian trend in Muslim-majority countries is the unvaried right of husbands to beat their wives; the differences of opinion are generally only on the extent of physicality that may be used in such discipline.

Verses in the Qur'an pertaining to women's dress (Q33:59, 24:31) have to do with the social structures of the time, in which women of rank covered their hair. The relevant Qur'anic verse here (24:31) instructs that the women should draw their head coverings over their cleavage. A later verse (33:59) instructs that they draw their mantles around them so that they might be recognized and not molested. The general exegesis of these verses is that the Muslim women were being instructed to dress like their counterparts in the other two Abrahamic faiths so that they might be recognized as adherents of a faith that had sexual morals and ethics that prohibited men from taking sexual liberties against them. After the death of Muhammad, and the conquest of other areas in the Middle East, it appears that the protocols regarding women's dress became more stringent. Along with covering of the face, and in some cases, the entire body (as is evident in the Afghan burqa), the women were increasingly secluded. In many societies, including France and other Western countries, the head covering is more of a political statement of identity rather than one to denote conservative values.

In this regard, Margot Badran writes that:

> Among the practices and institutions held to be Islamic but which are not required, nor perhaps even condoned by Islam, are segregation and seclusion of women, which have existed historically, and still do in some places, in urban areas of the Middle East, mainly among women of the upper and middle classes, although veiling, a distancing device, is practiced by lower-class women as well. Muslim societies took up the practices of the Byzantine and Sassanian worlds they conquered in the 7th century. Early in Islamic history, these practices came to be associated with Islam.
>
> (Badran 1988)

Islam and Violence

Islamic juridical reasoning uses the concept of *ta'lil* (ratiocination) in the Qur'an, wherein injunctions do not merely show divine authority, but they serve a purpose. As such, "when the effective cause, rationale and objective of a particular injunction are properly ascertained, these serve as basic indicators of the continued validity of the injunction" (Kamali 2006: 1:149–182). The Qur'an specifically provides the reasons for the women's covering at the time of Muhammad, and even though society has evolved to the point where, if society is supposedly Islamicate, sexual molestation ought not to occur, there seems to be a call for stricter rules on veiling. The argument is often conducted on Internet social media sites where opponents of the call for veiling often show photographs of Cairo, Iran, Iraq, and Kabul in the 1960s, in which most women are in public without head-dresses or mantles. Professor Abdullahi an-Na'im has noted that:

> In the last ten years, Islamist movements have sought to revive seclusion as an ideal for women. In direct response to the Soviet pressure to bring women out of the home, many Central Asian Muslims have come to regard veiling as the statement of anti-Russian nationalism. For example, in Uzbekistan, veiling has recently become common. Women who follow the opposition Wahabi movement have recently discarded the traditional and colourful Uzbek dress for full-body white veils as statements of recapturing religious/national identity.
> (an-Na'im 2002: 29)

The most stringent seclusion practices are known in Yemen, Saudi Arabia, Afghanistan, and Pakistan. These come with deleterious effects on education and employment. In Saudi Arabia and Yemen, while the system allows for the education of women, albeit in segregation, the Taliban instituted a seclusion that closed girls' schools, prohibited the use of makeup, and made the wearing of the burqa mandatory (an-Na'im 2002: 29). Girls and adult women who attempt to attend schools have been the targets of assaults, perhaps the most famous case being that of Malala Yusufzai, who was shot and left for dead. Her subsequent rescue and recovery, as well as a scholarship to study at Oxford, has catapulted her onto the world stage, which she now effectively uses to draw attention to the plight of women not only in Afghanistan, but in all part of the world where females encounter similar problems.

In terms of testimony specifically related to debts, Qur'an 2:282 advises: "And call upon two of your men to act as witnesses; and if two men are not available, then a man and two women from among such as are acceptable to you as witnesses, so that if one of the women errs, the other may remind her" (2:282). Given the conditions of the time, in which men were more engaged in business and more familiar with recording of such matters, the women's testimony would be a last resort. As Dr. Taha al-Alwani, former professor of Islamic legal theory at Muhammad bin Saud Islamic University, has noted, a deeper reading of the verse shows that "[t]he relevant wording implies that in general, transactions were not often matters of concern to women at that time. It also indicates that the actual witness would be one woman, even though her testimony might require the support of another woman who would 'remind' her if necessary. Thus, one woman acts as a guarantor for the accuracy of the other's testimony" (al-Alwani n.d.).

Classical Islamic understanding, however, does not know such deeper reflections; relying on the hadith refraction of Qur'anic verses, the general understanding takes what is actually a reprieve for women and makes it into a liability. During their monthly menstrual periods, women are exempt from prayer. Considering that a believing Muslim has to accept that the menstrual cycle is by divine decree, and not within the control of the woman, it would seem truly egregious to blame women for this occurrence. Yet there are several versions of a hadith that basically indicates that the Prophet, at one of the Eid commemorations in Islam, exhorted the people to give alms. When he passed by the women, he said to them,

> "O women! Give alms, for indeed I saw you as the majority of the people of the Hellfire!" They asked, "And what is the case for that, O messenger of God?" He responded, "You frequently curse, you are ungrateful to your husbands. I have not seen more deficient in intellect and religion, or those who cause a sensible man to go astray than one of you." They said, "What is the deficiency in our religion and our intellect, O messenger of God?" He responded, "Is not the testimony of a woman equal to half that of a man?" They said, "That is so!" He said, "That is her deficiency in intellect. Is it not that if she is on her monthly period, she may not pray nor fast?" They again said, "That is so!" He said, "And that is the deficiency of her religion!"
>
> (al-Bukhari 1999: 53)

This hadith clearly is at odds with the spirit of the scripture, but the classical approaches of hadith put the narrative in the category of "authentic" (*Sahih*), based on the probity of the narrators rather than an objective examination of the text. As such, Shaykh Muhammad Salih al-Munajjid, one of the most influential thinkers in Saudi Arabia, rather than condemn the hadith, tries to mansplain it away with the following:

> This does not mean that her reason is lacking entirely, or that her religious commitment is lacking entirely, rather the Messenger (peace and blessings of God be upon him) explained that the lack in her reasoning has to do with what may happen of her testimony

not being accurate, and the lack in her religious commitment has to do with what may happen of her missing prayers and fasts at the time of menses and *nifaas* (the period during which post-parturition bleeding occurs). But that does not imply that she is less than a man in everything, or that a man is better than her in everything.

Yes, the male gender is superior to the female gender in general, for many reasons, as Allah says (interpretation of the meaning):

"Men are the protectors and maintainers of women, because Allah has made one of them to excel the other, and because they spend (to support them) from their means" [al-Nisa' 4:34].

(al-Munajjid 2008a)

Perhaps the most painful evidence of the patriarchy as a conduit of violence concerns issues relating to sex, such as intercourse and the genitalia. In parts of the Middle East, Asia, and Africa, varying levels of female circumcision or infibulation are still practiced. While it is not specific to Muslims, on a global scale, the largest number of victims are Muslim women. Those who argue for it as a part of Islam rely on the hadith, custom, and a specious interpretation of Islamic law. There are some hadiths on the subject, two of the major ones being, "if the circumcised part (of a man) touches the circumcised part (of a woman), a bath becomes obligatory" (Wensinck and Mensing 1943: 2:11). Another hadith states that the Prophet advised a woman who was known to perform the service to not cut too severely. For some, "custom has the weight of law" in Islam, and as such, if the dominant practice of a people is circumcision for women, then such a custom is allowable, especially since in some areas, an uncircumcised woman is seen as more desirable (Abu Sahlieh 1994). Shaykh Jad al-Haqq, former rector of al-Azhar, relied on the concept that if something is not expressly forbidden, then it is allowable. As such, he ruled in favor of the practice (Abu Sahlieh 1994).

What seems evident is that the female, on one hand, is considered a source of desires that need to be controlled, and that this practice is supposed to fulfill that purpose. Another aspect is that the focus on virginity and purity is so obsessive that, in the more extreme cases, a woman's vaginal opening is sewn shut, with an opening left for the flow of menstrual blood and urination. While there is much literature about the negative aspects of the practice, it remains widespread.

The sexuality of the woman is so controlled in many Muslim-majority countries that the passing of *hudood* laws (done in Pakistan in 1977) and the confusion between rape and adultery in many such places only abet in the further victimization of rape victims. Classical Islamic law says that accusations of sexual promiscuity must be testified to by four witnesses of probity. The aim of this edict was to prevent people from making false accusations to besmirch the character of innocent people. Some jurists have made a connection between rape and adultery in which both sexual acts are placed on the same plane, without taking into consideration that one is by coercion and the other by consent. In the case of Pakistan, for example, the *hudood* laws place rape under what is known as *zina bil jabr* (literally sex outside of marriage by force). The law further states that:

> A person is said to commit *zina-bil-jabr* if he or she has sexual intercourse with a woman or man to whom he or she is not validly married, in any of the following circumstances, namely:
> a) Against the will of the victim;
> b) Without the consent of the victim;
> c) With the consent of the victim, when the consent has been obtained by putting the victim in fear of death or of hurt; or

d) With the consent of the victim, when the offender knows that the offender is not validly married to the victim and that the consent is given because the victim believes that the offender is another person to whom the victim is or believes herself or himself to be validly married.
   (Quraishi 1999: 403–431)

While all of these cases may be considered rape – as they would be in most Western courts of law – a problem comes up with the proof required to establish such rape:

Proof of *zina* or *zina-bil-jabr* liable to *hadd* shall be in one of the following forms:
a) The accused makes before a court of competent jurisdiction a confession of the commission of the offence; or
b) At least four Muslim adult witnesses, about whom the court is satisfied, having regard to the *tazkiyya al-shuhood* (credibility of witnesses), that they are truthful persons and abstain from major sins (*kabā'ir*), give evidence as eye-witnesses of the act of penetration necessary to the offence.
   (Quraishi 1999: 403–431)

The result is that many women have been punished for being raped. In other jurisdictions, where there may not be such confusions, the patriarchal attitudes still result in further assault against the victims. One such instance is known as the *Qatif* case, in which a rape victim was sentenced to imprisonment and being lashed in public. Her fault was that the rape occurred because she allowed herself to be in seclusion with a man who was not her male relative, a situation that is deemed a crime in Saudi Arabia (Setrakian 2007). The *hudood* laws in Pakistan basically demand that rape victims produce four witnesses to testify that they were in fact raped. If they cannot do this, then what exists is the fact that they have engaged in sexual activity, and this, outside of the bonds of marriage, must be punished.

The structure of Q24:2 is often seen as indicating that the woman is more answerable for her sexual conduct than a man since the verse reads: "And for the female fornicator and the male fornicator." The Qur'an, in this interpretation, puts the female first because in her case, supposedly, the wrongdoing is more egregious since she is supposed to be secluded in her home. The issue here is not whether that reading is correct or incorrect; the point is that sexual honor, either of the family or of the tribe, is seen to reside with the woman. Her breaking rules can lead to the dishonor of the entire clan, family, or tribe. As such, while honor killings are not part of the Qur'an or hadith, they are practiced in certain Muslim-majority states. Articles that allow honor killings exist in the legal code of most Arab countries. The Jordanian Penal Code, for example, No 16 (1960), article 340, states in part: "He who catches his wife, or one of his female unlawfuls committing adultery with another and he kills, wounds or injures one or both of them, is exempt from any penalty" (Abu Odeh 1996: 141–194).

The foregoing issues essentially infantilize women and make it easy to understand the controversy over females having positions of leadership in a mosque or other social setting. While the general rule in the Sharia is that of permissibility unless specifically prohibited (Q6:119 and 2:229), the appeal is often to the hadith that implies prohibition. According to one narration, the Prophet supposedly said that a woman should not lead the prayer (al-San'ānī n.d. 2:63). In his analysis of related traditions, it turns out that the matter is not clearly defined. Some classical jurists, such as al-Tabari and Abu Thawr, relied on other hadiths that indicate the Prophet allowed a woman to lead prayer (al-San'ānī n.d. 2:63). When Dr. Amina Wadud led the Friday prayer in South Africa in 2005, one of the Middle East's most famous scholars, Yusuf al-Qaradawi, deemed her action as un-Islamic and heretical (Abou El-Fadl 2006: viii). There are some female imams, but these are located in major cities in Western countries. China, however, has had a 300-year tradition of women's-only mosques led by female imams, but this occurrence seems specific to that country (Lim 2010).

Concomitant with the argument over women's leadership is their right to travel without a chaperone. The Prophet is supposed to have ruled that for a journey longer than three days, a female should be accompanied by a male relative (as reported in several hadiths; see also al-Munajjid 2008b). While many Muslim organizations still decree against a woman traveling alone, the general tone is toward a moderate interpretation, given the relative safety of modern transportation and security.

For some Muslims, as noted by Abdullah an-Na'im, it is women's issues and family law that is the battleground for control of the religion (2002: 91). Many – even if they don't identify as extremists – see the rights and freedom advocated by the Western bloc nations as going against the divine order and resulting in moral and ethical decay (an-Na'im 2002: 91). Several Muslim authors argue against patriarchal interpretations and offer new hermeneutical approaches to the scripture and tradition. Among the most famous are Fatima Mernissi, Amina Wadud, Leila Ahmed, Azizah al-Hibri, and Rifat Hasan. The problem is that their writings are accepted by a certain ilk that may be considered elitist or progressive, and not among the majority. Women such as Farhat Hashmi espouse the predominant androcentric viewpoint and are granted the resources to ensure that their material is more easily available to the masses. Whereas one has to purchase the books of those who argue against patriarchal interpretations, the literature that seeks to debate their ideas is often available free of charge, or via funded programs from established Muslim organizations. Patriarchy remains the status quo in institutional Islam.

Conclusion

From the very beginning of this work, I decided to show that although Islam falls under the rubric of religion, it transcends that limitation. Rather than use the standard confessional mantra of Islam meaning "submission to God," I showed that a more accurate interpretation is to place the word in the context of the Qur'an's intertextual relationship with Genesis 17:1, in which God orders Abraham to be perfect. The Hebrew imperative תָּמִים (*Tamim*) had become שְׁלִים (*Shlaim*) in the Targum. In the Qur'an's rendering of the narrative, the Arabic أسلم (*Aslim*) is used, and it is this context that the term must be understood as "seeking perfection." Islam, per Qur'anic directive (Q6:162), fits aptly into Peter Berger's coinage of a "sacred canopy," providing the basis of meaning and authority for everything a Muslim is supposed to do (Berger 1990). As such, even when a Muslim describes Islam as a religion, she is not referring to any self-evident category that separates it from the secular.

Most works after 9/11 focus on violence as assaults, killings, beheadings, torture, kidnappings, rapes, war, and terrorism. I opted for Craig Nessan's definition: "the attempt of an individual or group to impose its will on others through any nonverbal, verbal, or physical means that inflict psychological or physical injury" (Nessan 1998: 451). This allowed me to cover both the physical and psychological dimensions as found in jihad, law, and patriarchal interpretations of Islam. To stay within the parameters of the Cambridge Elements series, I did not cover certain aspects of violence, such as the destruction of buildings and statues, sacrificial rituals, and punishment in a Hereafter.

Many theorists show that apocalyptic beliefs are a source of religious violence (Juergensmeyer 1992: 106–111; Selengut 2003: 95–139). Apart from the messianic terminology of the Mahdist revolt in the Sudan (as outlined in Section 2) in the nineteenth century, I have not found any other major movements in Islam resorting to the concept. No major Muslim groups are trying to wage wars that hasten the coming of any messianic figure, although many do use the narratives about end-of-time tribulations to explain the present condition of some Muslim communities. Muqtada al-Sadr did employ apocalyptic imagery, leading the first organized armed resistance against United States in Najaf and Sadr City in 2004 as head of the *Jaysh al-Mahdi* (Army of the Mahdi). By 2008, however, amidst internal squabbling among various factions, he announced that he would renounce violence (Cochrane 2009). He founded the Sa'iroon Alliance that, in the May 12, 2018, parliamentary elections, won 54 of the 329 seats available. On August 19, 2018, the Iraqi Supreme Court ratified the results, meaning that Muqtada al-Sadr will play a major role in Iraqi politics. It seems that he has indeed given up resorting to violence, and it will be interesting to see how he charts a leadership course that objects to foreign influence on Iraqi affairs.

The Qur'an contains no end-of-time battle imagery, although it does mention Gog and Magog, figures associated with the prophesied wars in the books of Ezekiel and Revelations of the Hebrew and Christian Testaments. It is in the hadith that one finds narratives about the wars to come and the appearance of Jesus and the Mahdi, under headings like "Corruption and the Signs of the Final Hour" (Mohammed 1997). Even though the famous hadith scholar Ahmad ibn Hanbal (d. 855) noted that there are three types of oral traditions that are deemed baseless – those of wars, trials toward the end of time, and exegetical narratives – many Muslims still believe in those traditions (al-Zarkashi 2001: 2:173). Mirza Ghulam Ahmad (d. 1908) of the

Ahmadiyya sect relied on eschatological messianism hadiths to establish his authority, but repudiated jihad as meaning anything related to physical warfare.

There is, however, a psychological aspect of violence in "Signs of the Final Hour" narratives, in that they are often used to promote Judeophobia. A typical example is the following hadith, reported in *Sahih Muslim*:

> The last hour will not come unless the Muslims will fight against the Jews and the Muslims would kill them until the Jews would hide themselves behind a stone or a tree and a stone or a tree would say: Muslim, or servant of Allah, there is a Jew behind me; come and kill him; but the tree Gharqad would not say, for it is the tree of the Jews.
>
> (Ibn al-Hajjaj 1992: 4:1510)

The three major monotheist religions and their offshoots all use the story of Abraham's sacrifice to show that one ought to love God more than oneself. This certainly may be an excellent value, but the underlying imagery where we must admire someone who was willing to murder his own child at the behest of a God who thought such would be a fitting test depicts violence at its worst. This narrative brings to mind Jack Nelson-Pallmeyer's astute observation: religious violence is first and foremost, a problem of "sacred text," not a misinterpretation of sacred text (Nelson-Pallmeyer 2003: 20).

Charles Selengut has explained the ease with which religious people can resort to violence because of the unique nature of faith (Selengut 2008: 5–6). Emile Durkheim's definition of the idea of the sacred as "that which is set part and forbidden" also explains the ease with which religious actors commit violence (Durkheim 1965: 62). This would apply to the case of Islam in particular, wherein God is the all-Wise, all-Knowing, and thus, divine injunctions are outside of fallible human societal rules and conventions, and they are not open to question for those who truly consider themselves as committing to doing the will of God.

Islam, notwithstanding the proclamations of some apologists, is clearly not pacifist, as evidenced by the Qur'anic verses that exhort to fighting as circumstances may demand. Peace and pacifism may be the ideal, but these are only possible, at least from the perspective of the Abrahamic religions, with the imposition of monotheism. The conflicting dualism of the monotheist paths, wherein the forces of good and evil are incompatible and always in confrontation, makes violence inevitable. That violence may be purely psychological, and irenic exegetes may point out that the Qur'an contains many verses that endorse pluralism. None of this, however, can obfuscate the discriminatory binary construct of a righteous "us" and – at best – a tolerated "them."

The demonization of Islam, the invasion of Muslim-majority nations, regime changes, funding revolutions, or embargoes against them all lead to conditions that fall under a broad interpretation of the SMT, which can "transfer grievances into activism" (Gregg 2013). After 2001, when anti-Islamic rhetoric increased in the United States, religious parties in Afghanistan that had never gained more than 15–20% of the vote entered elections with a new manifesto: they would defend the honor of Islam (Ahmed 2007: 214). They ended up with landslide victories, unseating those who were once deemed unbeatable. They quickly allied themselves with the Taliban and elements of al-Qaeda to provide a major threat to Western forces.

The inequality of power means that Muslim-majority nations or Muslim citizens in non-Muslim-majority countries see themselves as besieged. This leads to what Akbar Ahmed calls a "post-honor World," wherein Muslims perceive that the honor of Islam is being threatened (Ahmed 2003: 56). The only way to protect this honor is to respond with violence that, in the face of the military superiority of the perceived enemy, legitimates the use of terrorism as an equalizer. That sense of being under siege also leads to a fanaticism that manifests itself in rigid interpretations of scripture and the need to return to an imagined "Islamic" past. The duty then is to recover that utopian past in which women must know their places, and where true believers, with the right understanding and enforcement of divine and prophetic edicts, will return Islam to its rightful glory. This mind-set has led to what Scott Appleby (2002: 85–92) and Khalid Abou El-Fadl (2014: 119) term the "vulgarization of Islam." Self-styled scholars or nonspecialists have become the voices of authority, creating an imagined, highly artificial Islam that emphasizes an incompatible "us" and "them" binary. I have not proposed any solutions because my goal has been simply to indicate the connection between Islam and violence. It is possible that solutions to some more overt forms of violence may be negotiated. Divesting any Abrahamic path – especially Islam – of all forms of violence would mean the undertaking of a jihad that, in the present circumstances, seems unthinkable.

Works Cited

Abdel Haleem, M. 2010. "Quranic Jihad: A Linguistic and Contextual Analysis," *Journal of Qur'anic Studies* 12, 147–166.

Abou El-Fadl, K. 2002. "The Place of Tolerance in Islam." In J. Cohen, I. Lague, and K. Abou El-Fadl (eds.). *The Place of Tolerance in Islam.* Boston, MA: Beacon Press, 3–26.

2006. "Foreword." In A. Wadud (ed.). *Inside the Gender Jihad.* London: Oneworld, vii–xiv.

2007. *The Great Theft.* New York, NY: Harper Collins.

2014. *Reasoning with God.* Lanham, MD: Rowman and Littlefield.

Abu, O. 1996. "Crimes of Honour and Construction of Gender in Arab Societies." In M. Yamani (ed.). *Feminism and Islam.* First edition. New York, NY: New York University Press, 141–194.

Abu Khalil, A. 1993. "A Note on the Study of Homosexuality in the Arab Islamic Civilization," *Arab Studies Journal* 1(2): 32–34, 48.

Abu Sahlieh, S. 1994. To Mutilate in the Name of Jehovah or Allah: Legitimization of Male and Female Circumcision. Available at: www.cirp .org/library/cultural/aldeeb1/#Religious. Accessed March 23, 2018.

Academy of Islamic Research. 1970. "Resolutions and Recommendations of the Fourth Conference of the Islamic Research Academy." In *The Fourth Conference of the Academy of Islamic Research, Conference Proceedings.* Cairo: General Organization for Government Printing Offices, 921–928.

Adang, C. 2003. "Ibn Hazm on Homosexuality," *Al Qantara* 24(1): 5–31.

Afsaruddin, A. 2007. "Views of Jihad throughout History," *Religion Compass* 1(1): 165–169.

2013. *Striving in the Path of God: Jihad and Martyrdom in Islamic Thought.* New York: Oxford University Press.

2015. "Early Competing Views on Jihad and Martyrdom." In E. Kendall and E. Stein (eds.). *Twenty-First Century Jihad: Law, Society and Military Action.* First edition. London: I. B. Tauris & Co. Ltd., 70–81.

2016. Jihad and Martyrdom in Islamic Thought and History. *Oxford Research Encyclopedia of Religion.* Available at: http://religion.oxfordre .com/view/10.1093/acrefore/9780199340378.001.0001/acrefore-9780199340378-e-46. Accessed April 13, 2018.

2017. "Orientalists, Militants and the Meanings of Jihad," *Renovatio* 1(1):43–47.

Ahmed, A. 2003. *Islam under Siege.* Cambridge: Polity Press.

2007. *Journey into Islam.* Washington, DC: Brookings Institute.

al-Albani, M. 2002. *Silsalat al-Ahādith al-Daīfa.* Riyadh: Maktabat al-Ma'ārif.

al-Alwani, T. n.d. The Testimony of Women in Islamic Law. Available at: www.alhewar.com/TahaTestimony.htm. Accessed March 23, 2018.

2011. *The Ethics of Disagreement in Islam.* Herndon, VA: International Institute of Islamic Thought.

Ali, K. 2013. *Sexual Ethics and Islam.* 4th Reprinting. London: Oneworld.

Alsumaih, A. 1998. *The Sunni Concept of Jihad in Classical Fiqh and Modern Islamic Thought.* School of Geography, Politics and Sociology. PhD Thesis. University of Newcastle upon Tyne.

Appleby, S. 2002. "The Quandary of Leadership." In J. Cohen, I. Lague, and K. Abou El-Fadl (eds.). *The Place of Tolerance in Islam.* Boston, MA: Beacon Press, 85–92.

Asad, T. 1993. *Genealogies of Religion: Discipline and Reasons of Power in Christianity and Islam.* Baltimore, MD: Johns Hopkins University Press.

Attia, G. 2007. *Towards Realization of the Higher Intents of Islamic Law.* London: International Institute of Islamic Thought.

Auda, J. June 28, 2015. "Same-sex marriages are not Islamically permissible, even if they are legally permissible." Jasser Auda: Facebook. Available at: www.facebook.com/notes/jasser-auda/same-sex-marriages-are-not-islamically-permissible-even-if-they-are-legally-perm/1048592735154037. Accessed March 23, 2018.

Avalos, H. 2005. *Fighting Words*. New York, NY: Prometheus Books.

Badran, M. 1988. Islam, Patriarchy and Feminism in the Middle East. *Women Living under Muslim Laws*. Available at: www.wluml.org/node/249. Accessed March 23, 2018.

Barlas, A. 2002. *Believing Women in Islam: Unreading Patriarchal Interpretations of the Qur'an*. Austin, TX: University of Texas Press.

Bearak, M. and D. Cameron. June 16, 2016. Here Are the 10 Countries Where Homosexuality May Be Punished by Death. www.washingtonpost.com/news/worldviews/wp/2016/06/13/here-are-the-10-countries-where-homosexuality-may-be-punished-by-death-2/?utm_term=.c023c47951c0. Accessed March 24, 2018.

Berger, P. 1990. *The Sacred Canopy: Elements of a Sociological Theory of Religion*. New York, NY: Anchor Books.

Bonner, M. 2006. *Jihad in Islamic History*. Princeton, NJ: Princeton University Press.

Bonney, R. 2004. *Jihad: From Qur'an to Bin Laden*. London: Palgrave Macmillan.

al-Bukhari, M. 1999. *Sahih Al-Bukhari*. Riyadh: Dar al-Salam Li-Nashr wa'l Tawzi'.

Casanova, J. 2011. "The Secular, Secularizations, Secularisms." In C. J. Calhoun, M. Juergensmeyer, and J. van Antwerpen (eds.). *Rethinking Secularism*. New York, NY: Oxford University Press, 54–74.

Cavanaugh, W. 2009. *The Myth of Religious Violence*. Oxford: Oxford University Press.

Chaudry, A. 2013. *Domestic Violence in the Islamic Tradition*. Oxford: Oxford University Press.

Churchill, W. 2004. *The River War: An Account of the Reconquest of Sudan*. London: Kessinger Publishing.

Clarke, P. 1982. *West Africa and Islam*. London: Edward Arnold.

Cochrane. M. 2009. Iraq Report #12: *The Fragmentation of the Sadrist Movement*. Institute for the Study of War. Available at: www .understandingwar.org/sites/default/files/Iraq%20Report%2012% 20Sadrist%20Movement%20Fragmentation.pdf. Accessed April 1, 2018.

Coulson, N. J. 1984. *A History of Islamic Law*. Edinburgh: Edinburgh University Press.

al-Dawoody, A. 2011. *The Islamic Law of War*. New York, NY: Palgrave Macmillan.

Denny, F. 1985. *An Introduction to Islam*. New York, NY: Macmillan Publishing Company.

Derrida, J. 2001. "On Forgiveness: A Roundtable Discussion with Jacques Derrida." In J. D. Caputo, M. Dooley, and M. J. Scanlon (eds.). *Questioning God*. First edition. Bloomington, IN: Indiana Press, 21–51.

Djait, H. 1978. *L'Europe et l'Islam*. Paris: Editions du Seuil.

Donner, F. 1981. *The Early Islamic Conquests*. Princeton, NJ: Princeton University Press.

1991. "The Sources of Islamic Conceptions of War." In J. Kelsay and J. Johnson (eds.). *Just War and Jihad*. First edition. New York, NY: Greenwood Press, 31–69.

2010. *Muhammad and the Believers at the Origins of Islam*. Cambridge, MA: Belknap Press of Harvard University Press.

Durkheim, E. 1965. *The Elementary Forms of Religious Life*. New York, NY: The Free Press.

Goitein, S. 1968. "A Plea for the Periodization of Islamic History." *Journal of the American Oriental Society* 88(2): 224–228.

Gouilly, A. 1952. *L'Islam dans l'Afrique Occidental Française*. Paris: Larose.

Gregg, H. 2013. Social Movements, Fundamentalism and Cosmic Warriors: Three Theories of Religious Activism and Violence. Available at: https://calhoun .nps.edu/bitstream/handle/10945/46762/Gregg_Social_movements_.pdf? sequence=1&isAllowed=y. Accessed April 6, 2018.

Hallaq, W. 1984. "Was the Gate of Ijtihad Closed?" *International Journal of Middle East Studies* 16(1): 3–41.

Harris, S. 2004. *The End of Faith*. New York, NY: W.W. Norton and Co. Ltd.

Hashmi, S. 1996. "Interpreting the Islamic Ethics of War and Peace." In T. Nardin (ed.). *The Ethics of War and Peace: Religious and Secular Perspectives*. First edition. Princeton, NJ: Princeton University Press, 146–168.

Hillenbrand, C. 2000. *The Crusades: Islamic Perspectives*. New York, NY: Routledge.

Hurgronje, S. 1916. *Mohammedanism*. New York, NY: G. P. Putnam and Sons.

Ibn al-Hajjaj, M. 1992. *Sahih Muslim*. Translated by A. H. Siddiqi. 4 volumes. Lahore: Sh. Muhammad Ashraf.

Ibn Athir, A. 1995. *Al-Kamil fi'Tarikh*. 13 volumes. Beirut: Dar al-Sadr.

Ibn Ishaq, M. 1986. *Al-Sirah al-Nabawiyyah*. Edited by 'Abd el-Ghaffar Sulayman al-Bindari. Beirut: Dar al-Kutub al-Ilmiyya.

Ibn Kathir, T. 1980. *Tafsir Ibn Kathir*. 4 volumes. Beirut: Dar al-Ma'rifa.

2003. *Al-Bidāya wa'l-Nihāya*. Edited by Ali Muhammad Mu'awwad and Adil Hamid Abd al-Mawjūd. Beirut: Dar al-Kutub al Ilmiyya.

Ibn Manzoor, M. n.d. *Lisan al-Arab*. 18 volumes. Beirut: Dar Ihya al-Turath al-'Arabi.

Ibn Sa'd, A. 1983. *Al-Tabaqāt al-Kubra*. Medina: al-Majlis al-'Ilmi.

Ibn Taimiyya, A. 2000. *Majmu' al-Fatāwa*. Compiled by A. Ibn Qasim. 37 volumes. Mecca: al-Nahdat al-Hadītha.

Works Cited

Jahangir, J. and H. Abdul Latif. 2015. *Islamic Law and Muslim Same-Sex Unions*. Lanham, MD: Lexington Books.

al-Jahiz, A. 1957. *Kitab Mufakharat Al-Jawari wa'-l-Ghilman*. Edited by C. Pellat. Beirut: Dar al-Makshuf.

Jastrow, M., J. McCurdy, and J. McDonald. 1906. "Ba'al and Ba'al Worship." *Jewish Encyclopedia*. Available at: www.jewishencyclopedia.com/articles/2236-ba-al-and-ba-al-worship. Accessed March 23, 2018.

Juergensmeyer, M. 1992. "Sacrifice and Cosmic War." In M. Juergensmeyer (ed.), *Violence and the Sacred in the Modern World*. First edition. New York, NY: Routledge, 106–111.

Juergensmeyer, M., M. Kitts, and M. Jerryson. 2013. "Introduction: The Enduring Relationship of Religion and Violence." In M. Juergensmeyer, M. Kitts, and M. Jerryson (eds.). *The Oxford Handbook of Violence and Religion*. First edition. Oxford: Oxford University Press, 1–14.

al-Juraysi, K. Compiler. 2007. *Al-Fatawa al-Shari'a fil' Masa'il al-Asriyya min Ulama al-Balad al-Haram*. Riyadh: Khalid al-Juraysi.

Kabbani, M. and S. Hendricks. n.d. Jihad: A Misunderstood Concept from Islam. Available at: http://islamicsupremecouncil.org/understanding-islam/legal-rulings/5-jihad-a-misunderstood-concept-from-islam.html. Accessed March 24, 2018.

Kafadar, C. 1995. *Between Two Worlds: The Construction of the Ottoman States*. Berkeley, CA: University of California Press.

Karsh, E. 2006. *Islamic Imperialism*. New Haven, CT: Yale University Press.

Keddie, N. 1994. "The Revolt of Islam, 1700 to 1993: Comparative Considerations and Relations to Imperialism," *Comparative Studies in Society and History* 36(3): 463–487.

Kennedy, C. 1996. *Islamization of Laws and Economy: Case Studies on Pakistan*. Islamabad, Pakistan: Institute of Policy Studies.

Works Cited

Khadduri, M. 1984. *The Islamic Conception of Justice*. Baltimore, MD: Johns Hopkins University Press.

Kimball, C. 2002. *When Religion Becomes Evil*. San Francisco, CA: Harper San Francisco.

Kugle, S. 2007. "Sexual Diversity in Islam." In V. Cornell, G. Henry, and O. Safi (eds.). *Voices of Islam*. 5 volumes. First edition. New York, NY: Praeger Press, 131–168.

    2010. *Homosexuality in Islam: Critical Reflections on Gays, Lesbians and Transgender Muslims*. Oxford: Oneworld Publications.

Labi, N. May 2007. The Kingdom in the Closet. Available at: www.theatlantic .com/magazine/archive/2007/05/the-kingdom-in-the-closet/305774/. Accessed March 23, 2018.

Lawrence, B. 1998. *Shattering the Myth*. Princeton, NY: Princeton University Press.

    2013. "Muslim Engagement with Injustice and Violence." In M. Juergensmeyer, M. Kitts, and M. Jerryson (eds.). *The Oxford Handbook of Violence and Religion*. First edition. Oxford: Oxford University Press, 128–151.

Lewis, B. 1988. *The Political Language of Islam*. Chicago, IL: Chicago University Press.

Lim, L. July 21, 2010. Female Imams Blaze Trail Amid China's Muslims. NPR Radio. Available at: www.npr.org/2010/07/21/128628514/female-imams-blaze-trail-amid-chinas-muslims. Accessed March 23, 2018.

Mamdani, M. 2004. *Good Muslim, Bad Muslim*. New York, NY: Pantheon Books.

al-Maqdisi, A. (More commonly referenced by the patronymic Ibn Quddama.) 2003. *Rawdat al-Nāẓir fi Jannat al-Manāẓir*. 3 volumes. Beirut: Dar al-Kutub al-Ilmiyya.

McAdam, K., J. McCarthy, and M. Zald. 1996. *Comparative Perspectives on Social Movements: Political Opportunities, Mobilizing Structures, and Cultural Framings.* New York, NY: Cambridge University Press.

Meek, C. 1925. *The Northern Tribes of Nigeria.* London: Oxford University Press.

Mohammed, K. 1997. *The Jewish and Christian Influences in the Eschatological Imagery of Sahih Muslim.* Department of Religion, Concordia University. M.A. Thesis. Montreal: Concordia University.

2001. Development of an Archetype: Studies in the Shurayh Traditions. Ph.D. Dissertation. McGill University.

2017. "Sex, Sexuality and the Family." In A. Rippin and J Mojaddedi (eds.). *The Wiley Blackwell Companion to the Qur'ān.* Second edition. Hoboken, NJ: Wiley Blackwell, 365–375.

Moosa, E. 2009. "Colonialism and Islamic Law." In M. Masud, A. Salvatore, and M. Bruinessen (eds.). *Islam and Modernity.* First edition. Edinburgh: Edinburgh University Press, 158–181.

Mottahadeh, R. and R. al-Sayyid. 2001. "The Idea of Jihad in Islam before the Crusades." In A. Laiou and R. Mottahadeh (eds.). *The Crusades from the Perspective of Byzantium and the Muslim World.* First edition. Washington, DC: Dumbarton Parks Research Library and Collection, 23–29.

al-Munajjid, S. 2008a. Meaning of the Lack of Reason and Religious Commitment in Women. Available at: https://islamqa.info/en/111867. Accessed March 23, 2018.

2008b. Travelling without a Mahram in Case of Necessity. Available at: https://islamqa.info/en/122630. Accessed March 23, 2018.

al-Nafzawi, M. 1990. *Al-Rawd al-'Atir fi Nuzhat al-Khātir.* Edited by J. Juma. London: Riyad el-Rayyes Books.

Nafzawi, U. 1963. *The Perfumed Garden.* Translated by R. Burton. London: Neville Spearman Publishers.

an-Na'im, A. Editor. 2002. *Islamic Family Law in a Changing World*. New York, NY: Zed Books.

an-Na'im, A. 2013. Islam and the Secular State: Rethinking Apostasy and Shari'a. Available at: www.abc.net.au/religion/articles/2013/05/13/3757780.htm. Accessed March 23, 2018.

Nelson-Pallmeyer, J. 2003. *Is Religion Killing Us? Violence in the Bible and the Quran*. Harrisburg, PA: Continuum.

Nessan, C. 1998. "Sex, Aggression, and Pain: Sociobiological Implications for Theological Anthropology," *Zygon* 33(3): 443–454.

Pape, R. 2005. *Dying to Win: The Strategic Logic of Suicide Terrorism*. New York, NY: Random House.

Pew Research Center. July 26, 2017. U.S. Muslims Concerned about Their Place in Society but Continue to Believe in the American Dream. Available at: http://assets.pewresearch.org/wp-content/uploads/sites/11/2017/07/09105631/U.S.-MUSLIMS-FULL-REPORT-with-population-update-v2.pdf. Accessed March 23, 2018.

Quraishi, A. 1999. "Her Honour: An Islamic Critique of the Rape Provisions in Pakistan's Ordinance on Zina," *Islamic Studies*, 38(3): 403–431.

al-Qurtubi, M. 2000. *M. Al-Jami' li-Ahkam al-Qur'an*. 21 books in 11 volumes. Beirut: Dar al-Kutub al-Ilmiyya.

Rahman, F. 1979. *Islam*. Chicago, IL: University of Chicago Press.

Rakoczy, S. 2004. "Religion and Violence: The Suffering of Women," *Agenda: Empowering Women for Gender Equity*, 24(3): 29–35.

Robinson, G. 2017. "The Four Waves of Global Jihad." In *Middle East Policy* 24(3): 70–88.

Rowson, E. 1991. "The Effeminates of Early Medina," *Journal of the American Oriental Society* 3(4): 671–693.

Roy, O. April 13, 2017. Who Are the New Jihadis? *Guardian*. Available at: www.theguardian.com/news/2017/apr/13/who-are-the-new-jihadis. Accessed April 7, 2018.

Saeed, L., R. Martin, and S. Syed. 2014. "Historical Patterns of Terrorism in Pakistan," *Defense and Security Analysis* 30(3): 209–229.

al-San'ānī, M. n.d. *Subul al-Salām: Sharh Bulūgh al-Marām min Jam' Adillat al-Ahkām*. 4 volumes. Beirut: Dār al-Kutub al-Ilmiyya.

Selengut, C. 2003. *Sacred Fury*. Second edition. Lanham, MD: Rowman and Littlefield.

Setrakian, L. November 21, 2007. Exclusive: Saudi Rape Victim Tells Her Story. ABC News. Available at: http://abcnews.go.com/International/story?id=3899920&page=1. Accessed March 23, 2018.

Shackford, S. June 13, 2016. In America, Muslims Are More Likely to Support Gay Marriage than Evangelical Christians. Available at: https://reason.com/blog/2016/06/13/in-america-muslims-are-more-likely-to-su. Accessed March 23, 2018.

al-Shaf'ie, H. 2003. "Introduction," *Islamabad Law Review* 1(1, 2): 1–12.

al-Sijistani, Abu Da'ud. 1996. *Sunan Abu Da'ud*. 4 volumes. Beirut: Dar al-Kutub al-Ilmiyya.

Smith, W. C. 1991. *The Meaning and End of Religion*. Minneapolis, MN: Fortress Press.

al-Tabari, M. n.d. *Tarikh al-Tabari*. Beirut: Bayt al-Afkar al-Duwaliyya. 1980–1986. *Ikhtilaf al-Fuqaha*. Beirut: Dar al-Kutub al-Ilmiyya

al-Tahawi, A. 1971. *Ikhtilaf al-Fuqaha*. Islamabad: Ma'had al-Abhāth al-Islamiyya.

Tiersky, R. 2016. ISIS's Deadliest Weapon Is the Idea of Heaven. *Huffington Post*. Available at: www.huffingtonpost.com/ronald-tiersky/isiss-deadliest-weapon-is_b_12087084.html. Accessed April 14, 2018.

Works Cited

Tyan, E. 1960. "Djihād." *Encyclopedia of Islam*. Second edition. Leiden: Brill, 2:538–539.

Weber, M. 1991. *The Sociology of Religion*. Boston, MA: Beacon Press.

Wensinck, A. J. and J. P. Mensing. 1943. *Concordance et Indices de la Tradition Musulmane*. 8 volumes. Leiden: Brill.

al-Zarkashi, B. 2001. *Al-Burhan fi Ulum al-Qur'an*. Beirut: Dar al-Kutub al-Ilmiyya.

Cambridge Elements

Religion and Violence

James R. Lewis
University of Tromsø

James R. Lewis is Professor of Religious Studies at the University of Tromsø, Norway, and the author and editor of a number of volumes, including *The Cambridge Companion to Religion and Terrorism*.

Margo Kitts
Hawai'i Pacific University

Margo Kitts edits the *Journal of Religion and Violence* and is Professor and Coordinator of Religious Studies and East-West Classical Studies at Hawai'i Pacific University in Honolulu.

ABOUT THE SERIES

Violence motivated by religious beliefs has become all too common in the years since the 9/11 attacks. Not surprisingly, interest in the topic of religion and violence has grown substantially since then. This Elements series on Religion and Violence addresses this new, frontier topic in a series of ca. fifty individual Elements. Collectively, the volumes will examine a range of topics, including violence in major world religious traditions, theories of religion and violence, holy war, witch hunting, and human sacrifice, among others.

ISSNs: 2397-9496 (online), 2514-3786 (print)

Cambridge Elements

Religion and Violence

Printed in the United States
By Bookmasters